ROLAND PARKER

Mastering Game Development with Python

Learn, Develop, and Master Game Design with Leading Python Libraries From Pygame to Panda 3D

First edition

This book was professionally typeset on Reedsy.
Find out more at reedsy.com

Contents

1. Introduction to Game Development

Overview of Game Development
Game development is a multifaceted process that involves the creation of interactive digital entertainment. It blends art, storytelling, and technology to produce engaging experiences that entertain and challenge players. The journey from concept to playable game involves several stages, each requiring specific skills and tools.

At its core, game development encompasses the design, creation, and iteration of video games. This process can be divided into several key phases: conceptualization, pre-production, production, testing, and release. Each phase is crucial to delivering a polished and enjoyable game.

1. **Conceptualization:** This is where the game idea is born. Developers brainstorm game mechanics, narrative elements, and visual styles. This phase often involves creating a game design document (GDD) that outlines the game's concept, goals, and overall vision.
2. **Pre-Production:** During this phase, the game's design is refined. Detailed planning occurs, including creating prototypes, designing characters and environments, and establishing technical requirements. This stage is essential for setting clear goals and preparing for the actual development process.
3. **Production:** The production phase is where the bulk of the work happens. This involves coding, creating assets (such as graphics and sound), and integrating these elements into the game. Development teams work on implementing game mechanics, levels, and features based

on the design document.

4. **Testing:** Testing ensures that the game is free of bugs and runs smoothly. Quality assurance (QA) testers play the game to identify and report issues. This phase may also include user testing to gather feedback from players and make necessary adjustments.

5. **Release:** After testing and final adjustments, the game is released to the public. This phase involves marketing and distribution, making the game available on various platforms, and managing post-release support, such as patches and updates.

Key Concepts and Terminology

Understanding key concepts and terminology is crucial for anyone involved in game development. Here are some fundamental terms and ideas:

1. **Game Design:** The process of creating the rules, structure, and content of a game. Game designers focus on how the game will be played, what mechanics will be used, and how the game will engage players.

2. **Game Mechanics:** The rules and systems that define how a game operates. These include player actions, game objectives, and the interactions between different elements of the game.

3. **Gameplay:** The experience of playing the game. It encompasses the interaction between the player and the game mechanics, including the challenges, rewards, and overall enjoyment.

4. **Assets:** The various components used to create a game, such as graphics, sound effects, music, and 3D models. Assets are created by artists and sound designers and integrated into the game by developers.

5. **Engine:** A game engine is a software platform used to build and run games. It provides essential tools and features, such as rendering, physics, and scripting. Popular game engines include Unity, Unreal Engine, and Godot.

6. **Prototype:** An early version of a game or a game feature used to test concepts and mechanics. Prototypes help developers validate ideas and make adjustments before full-scale development begins.

7. **Level Design:** The process of creating the environments and challenges within a game. Level designers work on crafting spaces where players interact with the game mechanics and progress through the game.

8. **User Interface (UI):** The visual elements that allow players to interact with the game, such as menus, buttons, and HUD (Heads-Up Display). A well-designed UI enhances the player's experience by providing clear and intuitive controls.

9. **Artificial Intelligence (AI):** The programming of non-player characters (NPCs) to behave in a realistic and challenging manner. AI can range from simple behaviors, like following a path, to complex decision-making systems.

10. **Game Loop:** The central cycle of a game that handles input, updates game state, and renders graphics. The game loop ensures that the game runs smoothly and responds to player actions in real time.

Tools and Technologies

The tools and technologies used in game development are diverse and continually evolving. Here are some of the key components:

1. **Game Engines:** Game engines are the backbone of modern game development. They provide a comprehensive set of tools and features for creating games. Notable engines include:

- **Unity:** Known for its versatility and large community, Unity supports both 2D and 3D game development. It is widely used for creating games across various platforms, including mobile, PC, and consoles.
- **Unreal Engine:** Renowned for its high-quality graphics and powerful tools, Unreal Engine is popular for AAA games and projects requiring advanced visual effects.
- **Godot:** An open-source engine that offers a user-friendly interface and flexible scripting options. Godot is favored for its ease of use and lightweight design.

1. **Programming Languages:** Different game engines use various programming languages. Common languages include:

- **C#:** Used primarily with Unity, C# is known for its simplicity and efficiency in scripting game mechanics.
- **C++:** The primary language for Unreal Engine, C++ offers high performance and control over low-level programming.
- **Python:** Used in engines like Godot, Python is appreciated for its readability and ease of learning.

1. **Graphics and Design Tools:** Creating game assets requires specialized software:

- **Photoshop:** A widely used tool for creating and editing textures, sprites, and other 2D assets.
- **Blender:** An open-source 3D modeling and animation tool used for creating 3D models, animations, and visual effects.
- **Substance Painter:** A tool for texturing 3D models, allowing artists to paint detailed textures directly onto models.

1. **Sound Design Tools:** Audio is an integral part of games, and several tools are used for creating and editing sound effects and music:

- **Audacity:** An open-source audio editor used for recording and editing sound effects.
- **FMOD:** A sound engine that allows developers to integrate complex audio systems into their games.
- **Wwise:** A comprehensive audio middleware solution used to create adaptive audio experiences in games.

1. **Version Control Systems:** Managing game development projects often involves collaboration and version control:

- **Git:** A widely used version control system that helps manage changes to code and assets, track progress, and collaborate with team members.
- **Perforce:** A version control system specifically designed for large-scale projects, including game development.

1. **Integrated Development Environments (IDEs):** IDEs provide a workspace for coding and debugging:

- **Visual Studio:** A popular IDE for C++ and C# development, offering robust debugging and coding features.
- **PyCharm:** An IDE used for Python development, including game scripting in engines like Godot.

Game development is a dynamic field that requires a blend of creativity, technical skills, and a deep understanding of the tools and technologies available. By mastering these concepts and utilizing the right tools, developers can bring their game ideas to life and create memorable experiences for players.

2. Getting Started with Python for Game Development

Python is a versatile and powerful programming language widely used in various fields, including game development. Its simplicity and readability make it an excellent choice for both beginners and experienced developers. This chapter covers the basics of Python, essential libraries for game development, and an introduction to object-oriented programming (OOP) principles, which are fundamental for creating robust and maintainable game code.

Python Basics and Setup

1. Installing Python

Before diving into game development, you need to install Python on your computer. Python is available for Windows, macOS, and Linux. Follow these steps to install it:

- **Download Python:** Visit the official Python website at python.org and download the latest version of Python. The website typically offers installers for all major operating systems.
- **Run the Installer:** Execute the downloaded installer. On Windows, make sure to check the box that says "Add Python to PATH" before proceeding. This ensures that you can run Python from the command line.

- **Verify Installation:** After installation, open a terminal or command prompt and type python —version or python3 —version to verify that Python is correctly installed.

2. Setting Up a Development Environment

A good development environment enhances productivity and makes coding more efficient. Here are some steps to set up a Python development environment:

- **Integrated Development Environment (IDE):** Choose an IDE or text editor that suits your needs. Popular choices include:
- **PyCharm:** A powerful IDE specifically for Python, offering advanced features like code completion, debugging, and project management.
- **Visual Studio Code:** A lightweight and versatile editor with extensive support for Python through extensions.
- **Jupyter Notebook:** Ideal for experimenting with code snippets and visualizing results, though it's less suited for larger projects.
- **Package Management:** Python uses pip, a package manager for installing libraries and dependencies. Ensure pip is installed by running pip —version in your terminal.

3. Writing and Running Python Code

To get started with Python, you can write simple scripts and run them:

- **Hello World:** Create a new file called hello.py and add the following code:

```python
Copy code
print("Hello, world!")
```

- Run this script by navigating to its directory in the terminal and typing python hello.py.
- **Python Shell:** You can also interact with Python in real-time using the Python shell. Simply type python or python3 in your terminal to start the interactive interpreter.

Essential Libraries for Game Development

Python boasts a rich ecosystem of libraries that simplify game development. Here are some essential libraries you'll use when developing games:

1. Pygame

Pygame is a popular library for creating 2D games in Python. It provides tools for handling graphics, sound, and input. To get started with Pygame:

- **Installation:** Install Pygame using pip:

```bash
Copy code
pip install pygame
```

- **Basic Example:** Create a simple Pygame window with the following code:

```python
Copy code
import pygame
import sys

pygame.init()
```

```
screen = pygame.display.set_mode((800, 600))
pygame.display.set_caption("Pygame Window")

while True:
    for event in pygame.event.get():
        if event.type == pygame.QUIT:
            pygame.quit()
            sys.exit()

    screen.fill((0, 0, 0))
    pygame.display.flip()
```

2. Arcade

Arcade is a modern Python library for 2D game development. It's known for its ease of use and performance. To get started with Arcade:

- **Installation:** Install Arcade using pip:

```bash
Copy code
pip install arcade
```

- **Basic Example:** Create a simple Arcade window with the following code:

```python
Copy code
import arcade

class MyGame(arcade.Window):
    def __init__(self):
        super().__init__(800, 600, "Arcade Window")
```

```python
    def on_draw(self):
        arcade.start_render()
        arcade.draw_text("Hello, Arcade!", 200, 300,
        arcade.color.WHITE, 24)

game = MyGame()
arcade.run()
```

3. Panda3D

Panda3D is a powerful library for 3D game development in Python. It offers extensive features for rendering and game logic. To get started with Panda3D:

- **Installation:** Install Panda3D using pip:

```bash
bash
Copy code
pip install panda3d
```

- **Basic Example:** Create a simple Panda3D scene with the following code:

```python
python
Copy code
from panda3d.core import Point3
from direct.showbase.ShowBase import ShowBase

class MyApp(ShowBase):
    def __init__(self):
        ShowBase.__init__(self)
        self.scene = self.loader.loadModel("models/environment")
        self.scene.reparentTo(self.render)
```

```
        self.scene.setScale(0.25, 0.25, 0.25)
        self.scene.setPos(-8, 42, 0)

app = MyApp()
app.run()
```

Introduction to Object-Oriented Programming

Object-Oriented Programming (OOP) is a programming paradigm based on the concept of "objects," which are instances of "classes." OOP helps in organizing and managing complex codebases by modeling real-world entities and their interactions. Here's an introduction to OOP concepts relevant to game development:

1. Classes and Objects

- **Class:** A class is a blueprint for creating objects. It defines a set of attributes and methods that its objects will have. For example, you might create a Player class with attributes like health and score and methods like move() and attack().
- **Object:** An object is an instance of a class. It represents a specific entity created from the class blueprint. For example, an instance of the Player class might represent a player character in the game.

```python
python
Copy code
class Player:
    def __init__(self, name, health):
        self.name = name
        self.health = health

    def move(self, direction):
        print(f"{self.name} moves {direction}")
```

11

```
player1 = Player("Hero", 100)
player1.move("north")
```

2. Inheritance

Inheritance allows a class to inherit attributes and methods from another class. This helps in creating a hierarchy of classes and promotes code reusability.

- **Base Class:** The class being inherited from is called the base class or parent class.
- **Derived Class:** The class inheriting from the base class is called the derived class or child class.

```python
python
Copy code
class Enemy(Player):
    def __init__(self, name, health, damage):
        super().__init__(name, health)
        self.damage = damage

    def attack(self, target):
        print(f"{self.name} attacks {target} for {self.damage}
        damage")

enemy1 = Enemy("Goblin", 50, 10)
enemy1.attack("Hero")
```

3. Encapsulation

Encapsulation involves bundling the data (attributes) and methods that operate on the data into a single unit or class. It also involves restricting access to some of the object's components, which is often done using access modifiers.

- **Public:** Attributes and methods that are accessible from outside the class.

- **Private:** Attributes and methods that are not accessible from outside the class, typically prefixed with double underscores (e.g., __health).

```python
Copy code
class Player:
    def __init__(self, name, health):
        self.name = name
        self.__health = health

    def take_damage(self, amount):
        self.__health -= amount

    def get_health(self):
        return self.__health
```

4. Polymorphism

Polymorphism allows objects of different classes to be treated as objects of a common base class. It enables methods to be used interchangeably across different classes.

- **Method Overriding:** A derived class can override methods of its base class to provide specific functionality.

```python
Copy code
class Character:
    def attack(self):
        print("Character attacks")

class Warrior(Character):
    def attack(self):
        print("Warrior swings a sword")
```

```python
class Mage(Character):
    def attack(self):
        print("Mage casts a spell")

characters = [Warrior(), Mage()]
for character in characters:
    character.attack()
```

5. Abstraction

Abstraction involves creating abstract classes and methods that define common interfaces for derived classes. It helps in designing systems where specific implementations are hidden from the user.

- **Abstract Class:** A class that cannot be instantiated on its own and is meant to be subclassed. It can contain abstract methods that must be implemented by derived classes.

```python
Copy code
from abc import ABC, abstractmethod

class AbstractCharacter(ABC):
    @abstractmethod
    def attack(self):
        pass

class Archer(AbstractCharacter):
    def attack(self):
        print("Archer shoots an arrow")

archer = Archer()
archer.attack()
```

By understanding and utilizing these Python basics, libraries, and OOP principles, you'll be well-equipped to embark on your journey in game development. Python's simplicity, combined with the power of its libraries and the organizational benefits of OOP, makes it an ideal choice for creating engaging and maintainable games.

3. Introduction to Pygame

ygame is a powerful and easy-to-learn library for creating 2D games in Python. It provides a range of tools for handling graphics, sound, and input, making it a popular choice for both beginners and experienced game developers. This chapter will cover the essentials of Pygame, including an overview of the library, installation instructions, setting up a Pygame project, and understanding basic concepts such as surfaces, events, and timing.

Pygame Overview and Installation

1. What is Pygame?

Pygame is a cross-platform set of Python modules designed for writing video games. It provides functionalities to handle graphics, sound, and user input, facilitating the development of 2D games and multimedia applications. Pygame is built on top of the Simple DirectMedia Layer (SDL), which is a low-level library used for managing video, audio, and input.

Key features of Pygame include:

- **Graphics:** Pygame supports drawing shapes, images, and text on the screen. It provides functions for handling 2D graphics and managing game assets.
- **Sound:** Pygame includes modules for playing and manipulating sound effects and music, enhancing the multimedia experience of your game.
- **Input Handling:** It offers support for keyboard, mouse, and joystick

input, allowing players to interact with your game.

- **Timing:** Pygame has functions to manage game timing and frame rates, ensuring smooth and consistent gameplay.

2. Installing Pygame

To start using Pygame, you need to install it in your Python environment. Follow these steps:

- **Ensure Python is Installed:** Before installing Pygame, make sure Python is installed on your system. You can download Python from python.org.
- **Install Pygame via pip:** Pygame can be easily installed using pip, the Python package manager. Open a terminal or command prompt and run:

```bash
Copy code
pip install pygame
```

- This command will download and install the latest version of Pygame and its dependencies.
- **Verify Installation:** To check if Pygame is installed correctly, you can run a simple test. Open a Python interpreter and execute the following code:

```python
Copy code
import pygame
print(pygame.__version__)
```

- If Pygame is installed correctly, this command will print the installed version of Pygame.

Setting Up a Pygame Project

1. Creating a Project Structure

Organizing your project files is crucial for managing and developing your game efficiently. Here's a basic structure for a Pygame project:

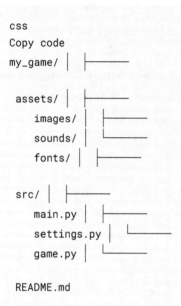

```
css
Copy code
my_game/ |  ├───────

   assets/ |  ├───────
     images/ |  ├──────
     sounds/ |  └──────
     fonts/ |  ├──────

   src/ |  ├───────
     main.py |  ├──────
     settings.py |  └──────
     game.py |  └──────

README.md
```

- **assets/ Directory:** This folder contains game assets such as images, sound files, and fonts. Organize your assets into subdirectories for better management.
- **src/ Directory:** This is where your source code resides. It includes:
- main.py: The entry point of your game, responsible for initializing Pygame and running the game loop.
- settings.py: A module for storing configuration settings like screen dimensions and colors.
- game.py: The main game logic and classes.

- **README.md File:** A file for documenting your project, including instructions for running the game and any other relevant information.

2. Writing the Main Game Script

The main game script (main.py) is the entry point of your game. It initializes Pygame, sets up the game window, and starts the game loop. Here's a basic example:

```python
Copy code
import pygame
import sys

def main():
    # Initialize Pygame
    pygame.init()

    # Set up display
    width, height = 800, 600
    screen = pygame.display.set_mode((width, height))
    pygame.display.set_caption("My Game")

    # Main game loop
    clock = pygame.time.Clock()
    while True:
        # Handle events
        for event in pygame.event.get():
            if event.type == pygame.QUIT:
                pygame.quit()
                sys.exit()

        # Update game state

        # Draw to the screen
        screen.fill((0, 0, 0))  # Fill the screen with black
        pygame.display.flip()  # Update the display

        # Cap the frame rate
```

```
        clock.tick(60)

if __name__ == "__main__":
    main()
```

- **Initialization:** pygame.init() initializes all Pygame modules.
- **Display Setup:** pygame.display.set_mode() creates the game window, and pygame.display.set_caption() sets the window title.
- **Game Loop:** The loop handles events, updates the game state, and draws to the screen.
- **Event Handling:** The pygame.event.get() function retrieves all events, and checking pygame.QUIT handles the window close event.
- **Drawing:** screen.fill() clears the screen, and pygame.display.flip() updates the display.
- **Frame Rate:** clock.tick(60) limits the frame rate to 60 frames per second (FPS).

3. Adding Game Settings

A settings.py file can store game configuration settings. This helps in managing constants and adjusting settings without modifying the main game script. Here's an example:

```python
Copy code
# settings.py

# Screen settings
WIDTH = 800
HEIGHT = 600
TITLE = "My Game"
FPS = 60

# Colors
```

```
BLACK = (0, 0, 0)
WHITE = (255, 255, 255)
```

You can import these settings into your main.py:

```python
python
Copy code
import pygame
import sys
from settings import WIDTH, HEIGHT, TITLE, FPS, BLACK

def main():
    pygame.init()
    screen = pygame.display.set_mode((WIDTH, HEIGHT))
    pygame.display.set_caption(TITLE)
    clock = pygame.time.Clock()

    while True:
        for event in pygame.event.get():
            if event.type == pygame.QUIT:
                pygame.quit()
                sys.exit()

        screen.fill(BLACK)
        pygame.display.flip()
        clock.tick(FPS)

if __name__ == "__main__":
    main()
```

Basic Pygame Concepts: Surface, Events, and Timing

1. Surfaces

In Pygame, a surface is a fundamental concept representing any drawable object on the screen. Everything you see on the screen is drawn onto a surface. Here's an overview:

- **Screen Surface:** The main surface where everything is drawn. It is created using pygame.display.set_mode().
- **Surface Object:** You can create additional surfaces for images, shapes, or text using pygame.Surface().

Creating and Drawing Surfaces

To create a surface, use the pygame.Surface() constructor:

```python
Copy code
surface = pygame.Surface((width, height))
surface.fill((255, 0, 0))  # Fill the surface with red
```

To draw this surface onto the screen:

```python
Copy code
screen.blit(surface, (x, y))
```

The blit() method copies the content of one surface onto another. In this case, it draws the red surface onto the main screen surface.

Loading and Displaying Images

You can load images into surfaces using pygame.image.load():

```python
Copy code
image = pygame.image.load("assets/images/my_image.png")
```

To display the image:

```python
Copy code
screen.blit(image, (x, y))
```

2. Events

Events in Pygame represent user interactions and system messages. Handling events is crucial for making your game responsive to player input. Here's how to handle events:

Event Loop

Within the game loop, use pygame.event.get() to retrieve a list of all events:

```python
Copy code
for event in pygame.event.get():
    if event.type == pygame.QUIT:
        pygame.quit()
        sys.exit()
```

Handling Keyboard Input

To handle keyboard input, check for KEYDOWN and KEYUP events:

```python
Copy code
for event in pygame.event.get():
    if event.type == pygame.KEYDOWN:
        if event.key == pygame.K_LEFT:
            print("Left arrow key pressed")
```

Handling Mouse Input

Mouse events can be handled similarly:

```python
Copy code
for event in pygame.event.get():
    if event.type == pygame.MOUSEBUTTONDOWN:
        if event.button == 1:  # Left mouse button
            print("Mouse button clicked at", event.pos)
```

3. Timing

Timing is essential for managing game updates and maintaining a consistent frame rate. Pygame provides tools to control timing and frame rate.

Using the Clock

The pygame.time.Clock class helps manage the frame rate:

```python
Copy code
clock = pygame.time.Clock()
```

Call clock.tick(FPS) in the game loop to limit the frame rate:

```python
Copy code
clock.tick(60)  # 60 frames per second
```

Delta Time

To ensure smooth movement regardless of frame rate variations, use delta time:

```python
Copy code
last_time = pygame.time.get_ticks()
delta_time = (pygame.time.get_ticks() - last_time) / 1000.0
last_time = pygame.time.get_ticks()
```

Use delta_time to adjust movement:

```python
Copy code
player_x += player_speed * delta_time
```

Summary

Pygame provides a robust framework for developing 2D games in Python. By understanding its core concepts—surfaces, events, and timing—you can create interactive and engaging games. The library's simplicity and flexibility make it an excellent choice for both newcomers and experienced developers. As you continue to develop your game, you'll leverage these concepts to build and refine your game's mechanics, graphics, and user experience.

4. Building Your First Game with Pygame

Creating a game with Pygame involves several key steps, including setting up a game loop, handling user input, displaying graphics, and implementing game logic and state management. This chapter will guide you through building your first game with Pygame, focusing on these essential components.

Creating a Simple Game Loop

The game loop is the core of any game. It continually updates the game state, processes user input, and renders the graphics. A well-designed game loop ensures that your game runs smoothly and responds to player actions in real time. Let's break down the process of creating a simple game loop in Pygame.

1. Basic Structure of the Game Loop

Here's a basic structure for a game loop in Pygame:

```python
Copy code
import pygame
import sys

def main():
    # Initialize Pygame
    pygame.init()

    # Set up display
```

```
    width, height = 800, 600
    screen = pygame.display.set_mode((width, height))
    pygame.display.set_caption("My First Game")

    # Set up clock for managing frame rate
    clock = pygame.time.Clock()

    while True:
        # Handle events
        for event in pygame.event.get():
            if event.type == pygame.QUIT:
                pygame.quit()
                sys.exit()

        # Update game state

        # Draw to the screen
        screen.fill((0, 0, 0))  # Fill the screen with black
        pygame.display.flip()   # Update the display

        # Cap the frame rate
        clock.tick(60)

if __name__ == "__main__":
    main()
```

Explanation:

- **Initialize Pygame:** pygame.init() sets up all the Pygame modules.
- **Display Setup:** pygame.display.set_mode() creates the game window, and pygame.display.set_caption() sets the window title.
- **Clock for Frame Rate:** pygame.time.Clock() helps control the game's frame rate with clock.tick(60).
- **Event Handling:** The event loop checks for events like quitting the game.
- **Update and Draw:** The game state is updated, and the screen is redrawn every frame.
- **Frame Rate Management:** clock.tick(60) limits the frame rate to 60

FPS.

2. Adding a Game Object

Let's add a simple game object, such as a rectangle that moves across the screen. We will update the game loop to include this object and handle its movement.

```python
Copy code
import pygame
import sys

def main():
    pygame.init()
    width, height = 800, 600
    screen = pygame.display.set_mode((width, height))
    pygame.display.set_caption("My First Game")
    clock = pygame.time.Clock()

    # Define the player object
    player_color = (255, 0, 0)  # Red color
    player_size = 50
    player_x = width // 2
    player_y = height // 2
    player_speed = 5

    while True:
        for event in pygame.event.get():
            if event.type == pygame.QUIT:
                pygame.quit()
                sys.exit()

        # Handle input
        keys = pygame.key.get_pressed()
        if keys[pygame.K_LEFT]:
            player_x -= player_speed
        if keys[pygame.K_RIGHT]:
            player_x += player_speed
        if keys[pygame.K_UP]:
```

```
            player_y -= player_speed
        if keys[pygame.K_DOWN]:
            player_y += player_speed

        # Update game state

        # Draw to the screen
        screen.fill((0, 0, 0))  # Fill the screen with black
        pygame.draw.rect(screen, player_color, (player_x,
        player_y, player_size, player_size))
        pygame.display.flip()

        clock.tick(60)

if __name__ == "__main__":
    main()
```

Explanation:

- **Player Object:** A red rectangle that moves based on user input.
- **Input Handling:** Arrow keys are used to move the rectangle.
- **Drawing the Object:** pygame.draw.rect() draws the rectangle on the screen.

Handling Input and Displaying Graphics

1. Handling User Input

Handling user input is crucial for interactive games. Pygame provides several ways to capture and respond to user input, including keyboard and mouse events.

Keyboard Input

Pygame captures keyboard input using the pygame.key.get_pressed() function, which returns a list of boolean values representing the state of each key. You can check if specific keys are pressed and respond accordingly.

Here's an example of handling keyboard input:

```python
Copy code
keys = pygame.key.get_pressed()
if keys[pygame.K_LEFT]:
    # Move left
if keys[pygame.K_RIGHT]:
    # Move right
if keys[pygame.K_UP]:
    # Move up
if keys[pygame.K_DOWN]:
    # Move down
```

Mouse Input

You can also handle mouse input using pygame.mouse.get_pos() to get the current position of the mouse and pygame.mouse.get_pressed() to check the state of the mouse buttons.

Example of handling mouse input:

```python
Copy code
mouse_x, mouse_y = pygame.mouse.get_pos()
mouse_buttons = pygame.mouse.get_pressed()
if mouse_buttons[0]:  # Left mouse button
    # Handle left click
```

2. Displaying Graphics

Pygame offers various functions to draw shapes, images, and text on the screen.

Drawing Shapes

Pygame provides functions to draw basic shapes like rectangles, circles, and lines:

```python
Copy code
pygame.draw.rect(screen, color, (x, y, width, height))  # Draw
rectangle
```

```
pygame.draw.circle(screen, color, (x, y), radius)      # Draw circle
pygame.draw.line(screen, color, (start_x, start_y), (end_x,
end_y), width)  # Draw line
```

Displaying Images

To display images, you first need to load them into surfaces using pygame.image.load():

```python
Copy code
image = pygame.image.load("path/to/image.png")
screen.blit(image, (x, y))  # Draw the image on the screen
```

Rendering Text

Rendering text requires creating a font object and rendering text surfaces:

```python
Copy code
font = pygame.font.Font(None, 36)
text_surface = font.render("Hello, Pygame!", True, (255, 255, 255))
screen.blit(text_surface, (x, y))
```

Implementing Game Logic and State Management

1. Game State Management

Game state management involves keeping track of different states or stages in your game, such as the main menu, gameplay, and game over screens. You can manage game states using a simple state machine.

State Machine Example

Here's a basic implementation of a state machine:

```python
Copy code
```

```python
import pygame
import sys

# Define game states
MAIN_MENU = 0
PLAYING = 1
GAME_OVER = 2

def main():
    pygame.init()
    width, height = 800, 600
    screen = pygame.display.set_mode((width, height))
    pygame.display.set_caption("State Management Example")
    clock = pygame.time.Clock()

    # Initialize game state
    game_state = MAIN_MENU

    while True:
        for event in pygame.event.get():
            if event.type == pygame.QUIT:
                pygame.quit()
                sys.exit()

        # Handle game logic based on state
        if game_state == MAIN_MENU:
            screen.fill((0, 0, 0))  # Black background
            # Draw main menu elements
            font = pygame.font.Font(None, 36)
            text_surface = font.render("Main Menu - Press ENTER to
            Start", True, (255, 255, 255))
            screen.blit(text_surface, (width // 4, height // 2))

            keys = pygame.key.get_pressed()
            if keys[pygame.K_RETURN]:
                game_state = PLAYING

        elif game_state == PLAYING:
            screen.fill((0, 0, 0))  # Black background
            # Draw game elements
```

```
        pygame.draw.circle(screen, (255, 0, 0), (width // 2,
        height // 2), 50)

        keys = pygame.key.get_pressed()
        if keys[pygame.K_ESCAPE]:
            game_state = GAME_OVER

    elif game_state == GAME_OVER:
        screen.fill((0, 0, 0))  # Black background
        # Draw game over screen
        font = pygame.font.Font(None, 36)
        text_surface = font.render("Game Over - Press ESC to
        Exit", True, (255, 255, 255))
        screen.blit(text_surface, (width // 4, height // 2))

        keys = pygame.key.get_pressed()
        if keys[pygame.K_ESCAPE]:
            pygame.quit()
            sys.exit()

    pygame.display.flip()
    clock.tick(60)

if __name__ == "__main__":
    main()
```

2. Implementing Game Logic

Game logic refers to the rules and mechanics that govern gameplay. This includes updating game objects, handling collisions, and managing scores.

Updating Game Objects

In the game loop, update the positions and states of game objects based on user input and other game events:

```
python
Copy code
player_x += player_speed
enemy_x -= enemy_speed
```

Handling Collisions

To handle collisions between objects, you can use bounding boxes or more complex collision detection algorithms:

```python
Copy code
if player_rect.colliderect(enemy_rect):
    # Handle collision
```

Managing Scores

To keep track of scores, create a variable to store the score and update it based on game events:

```python
Copy code
score = 0

# Increase score
score += 10

# Display score
font = pygame.font.Font(None, 36)
score_surface = font.render(f"Score: {score}", True, (255, 255, 255))
screen.blit(score_surface, (10, 10))
```

Putting It All Together

To build a complete game, integrate all the concepts covered:

1. **Create the Game Loop:** Initialize Pygame, set up the display, and manage the game loop.
2. **Handle Input:** Capture and respond to user input from the keyboard and mouse.
3. **Display Graphics:** Draw game objects, backgrounds, and text on the screen.

4. **Implement Game Logic:** Update game objects, handle collisions, and manage game states.
5. **Manage States:** Use a state machine to handle different game screens and stages.

Here's an example of a simple game that combines these elements:

```python
Copy code
import pygame
import sys

# Define game states
MAIN_MENU = 0
PLAYING = 1
GAME_OVER = 2

def main():
    pygame.init()
    width, height = 800, 600
    screen = pygame.display.set_mode((width, height))
    pygame.display.set_caption("Simple Game Example")
    clock = pygame.time.Clock()

    # Initialize game state
    game_state = MAIN_MENU
    player_x, player_y = width // 2, height // 2
    player_speed = 5
    score = 0

    while True:
        for event in pygame.event.get():
            if event.type == pygame.QUIT:
                pygame.quit()
                sys.exit()

        keys = pygame.key.get_pressed()

        if game_state == MAIN_MENU:
```

```
    screen.fill((0, 0, 0))
    font = pygame.font.Font(None, 36)
    text_surface = font.render("Main Menu - Press ENTER to
    Start", True, (255, 255, 255))
    screen.blit(text_surface, (width // 4, height // 2))
    if keys[pygame.K_RETURN]:
        game_state = PLAYING

elif game_state == PLAYING:
    if keys[pygame.K_LEFT]:
        player_x -= player_speed
    if keys[pygame.K_RIGHT]:
        player_x += player_speed
    if keys[pygame.K_UP]:
        player_y -= player_speed
    if keys[pygame.K_DOWN]:
        player_y += player_speed

    screen.fill((0, 0, 0))
    pygame.draw.rect(screen, (255, 0, 0), (player_x,
    player_y, 50, 50))
    score += 1  # Example of increasing score
    font = pygame.font.Font(None, 36)
    score_surface = font.render(f"Score: {score}", True,
    (255, 255, 255))
    screen.blit(score_surface, (10, 10))
    if keys[pygame.K_ESCAPE]:
        game_state = GAME_OVER

elif game_state == GAME_OVER:
    screen.fill((0, 0, 0))
    font = pygame.font.Font(None, 36)
    text_surface = font.render(f"Game Over - Final Score:
    {score}", True, (255, 255, 255))
    screen.blit(text_surface, (width // 4, height // 2))
    if keys[pygame.K_ESCAPE]:
        pygame.quit()
        sys.exit()

pygame.display.flip()
```

```
        clock.tick(60)

if __name__ == "__main__":
    main()
```

Summary

Building your first game with Pygame involves understanding the game loop, handling user input, displaying graphics, and implementing game logic and state management. By following the steps outlined in this chapter, you can create a basic but functional game that serves as a foundation for more complex projects. As you gain experience, you can expand on these concepts to develop more sophisticated games with richer graphics, advanced gameplay mechanics, and engaging user experiences.

5. Advanced Pygame Techniques

As you delve deeper into game development with Pygame, you'll want to explore more advanced techniques to enhance your game's functionality and player experience. This chapter covers three key areas: sound and music integration, animations and sprite management, and collision detection and physics. Mastering these techniques will allow you to create more engaging and polished games.

Sound and Music Integration

1. Adding Sound Effects

Sound effects play a crucial role in making games immersive and engaging. Pygame provides support for loading and playing sound effects using its pygame.mixer module. Here's how you can integrate sound effects into your game:

Initializing the Mixer

Before using the pygame.mixer module, you need to initialize it:

```python
Copy code
pygame.mixer.init()
```

Loading and Playing Sound Effects

You can load sound files (e.g., WAV files) into pygame.mixer.Sound objects and play them:

```python
Copy code
# Load sound effect
sound_effect = pygame.mixer.Sound("assets/sounds/jump.wav")

# Play sound effect
sound_effect.play()
```

Controlling Sound Playback

You can control sound playback with various methods:

- **play()**: Plays the sound.
- **stop()**: Stops the sound.
- **pause()**: Pauses the sound.
- **unpause()**: Unpauses the sound.

Example of using these methods:

```python
Copy code
sound_effect.play()
pygame.time.wait(500)  # Wait for 500 milliseconds
sound_effect.stop()
```

2. Adding Background Music

Background music enhances the atmosphere of your game. Use pygame.mixer.music to handle background music tracks.

Loading and Playing Music

Load a music file (e.g., MP3 or OGG) and play it:

```python
Copy code
pygame.mixer.music.load("assets/music/background.mp3")
pygame.mixer.music.play(-1)  # -1 means loop indefinitely
```

Controlling Music Playback

You can also control music playback with various methods:

- **play()**: Plays the music.
- **pause()**: Pauses the music.
- **unpause()**: Unpauses the music.
- **stop()**: Stops the music.

Example:

```python
Copy code
pygame.mixer.music.pause()
pygame.time.wait(1000)  # Wait for 1 second
pygame.mixer.music.unpause()
```

3. Handling Volume

Control the volume of sound effects and music using the set_volume() method:

```python
Copy code
sound_effect.set_volume(0.5)  # Set volume to 50%
pygame.mixer.music.set_volume(0.3)  # Set background music volume to 30%
```

4. Advanced Sound Techniques

Sound Channels: Pygame provides multiple channels to play different sounds simultaneously.

```python
Copy code
channel = pygame.mixer.Channel(0)  # Use channel 0
channel.play(sound_effect)
```

Fade In/Out: Gradually fade in or out sound effects or music.

```python
Copy code
sound_effect.play(fade_ms=2000)  # Fade in over 2 seconds
pygame.mixer.music.fadeout(2000)  # Fade out music over 2 seconds
```

Animations and Sprite Management

1. Understanding Sprites

Sprites are images or animations used in games to represent characters, objects, or effects. Pygame provides the pygame.sprite.Sprite class and the pygame.sprite.Group class for managing sprites efficiently.

Creating Sprites

Create a custom sprite by subclassing pygame.sprite.Sprite:

```python
Copy code
import pygame

class Player(pygame.sprite.Sprite):
    def __init__(self):
        super().__init__()
        self.image =
        pygame.image.load("assets/images/player.png").convert_alpha()
        self.rect = self.image.get_rect()
        self.rect.center = (400, 300)

    def update(self):
        # Update sprite position or state
        keys = pygame.key.get_pressed()
        if keys[pygame.K_LEFT]:
            self.rect.x -= 5
        if keys[pygame.K_RIGHT]:
            self.rect.x += 5
        if keys[pygame.K_UP]:
```

41

```
        self.rect.y -= 5
    if keys[pygame.K_DOWN]:
        self.rect.y += 5
```

Using Sprite Groups

Sprite groups help manage multiple sprites efficiently. Add sprites to a group and update or draw them together:

```python
Copy code
all_sprites = pygame.sprite.Group()
player = Player()
all_sprites.add(player)

while True:
    for event in pygame.event.get():
        if event.type == pygame.QUIT:
            pygame.quit()
            sys.exit()

    # Update sprites
    all_sprites.update()

    # Draw sprites
    screen.fill((0, 0, 0))
    all_sprites.draw(screen)
    pygame.display.flip()
    clock.tick(60)
```

2. Implementing Animations

Animations are created by displaying a sequence of images in succession. This technique is often used for character movement or special effects.

Creating an Animation

To create an animation, load a sequence of images and cycle through them:

```python
Copy code
class AnimatedSprite(pygame.sprite.Sprite):
    def __init__(self):
        super().__init__()
        self.frames =
        [pygame.image.load(f"assets/images/frame_{i}.png").convert_alpha()
        for i in range(1, 5)]
        self.current_frame = 0
        self.image = self.frames[self.current_frame]
        self.rect = self.image.get_rect()
        self.rect.center = (400, 300)
        self.frame_rate = 10
        self.last_update = pygame.time.get_ticks()

    def update(self):
        now = pygame.time.get_ticks()
        if now - self.last_update > 1000 // self.frame_rate:
            self.last_update = now
            self.current_frame = (self.current_frame + 1) %
            len(self.frames)
            self.image = self.frames[self.current_frame]
```

3. Handling Sprite Collisions

Detecting and handling collisions between sprites is essential for interactive gameplay. Pygame provides methods for collision detection.

Rectangular Collisions

Use the colliderect() method to check if two rectangles intersect:

```python
Copy code
if pygame.sprite.collide_rect(sprite1, sprite2):
    # Handle collision
```

Pixel-Perfect Collisions

For more precise collision detection, use pygame.sprite.collide_mask():

43

```python
Copy code
if pygame.sprite.collide_mask(sprite1, sprite2):
    # Handle collision
```

4. Advanced Animation Techniques

Animation Timing: Control the speed of animations using frame rates and timing:

```python
Copy code
def update(self):
    now = pygame.time.get_ticks()
    if now - self.last_update > 1000 // self.frame_rate:
        # Update animation frame
```

Animation States: Manage different animation states for complex characters:

```python
Copy code
class Player(pygame.sprite.Sprite):
    def __init__(self):
        super().__init__()
        self.idle_frames =
        [pygame.image.load(f"assets/images/idle_{i}.png").convert_alpha()
        for i in range(1, 4)]
        self.run_frames =
        [pygame.image.load(f"assets/images/run_{i}.png").convert_alpha()
        for i in range(1, 6)]
        self.current_frames = self.idle_frames
        self.current_frame = 0
        self.image = self.current_frames[self.current_frame]
        self.rect = self.image.get_rect()
        self.frame_rate = 10
        self.last_update = pygame.time.get_ticks()
```

```
def update(self):
    # Update animation frames based on state
    now = pygame.time.get_ticks()
    if now - self.last_update > 1000 // self.frame_rate:
        self.last_update = now
        self.current_frame = (self.current_frame + 1) %
        len(self.current_frames)
        self.image = self.current_frames[self.current_frame]
```

Collision Detection and Physics

1. Basic Collision Detection

Collision detection is crucial for detecting interactions between game objects, such as characters, enemies, and obstacles.

Rectangular Collisions

Use the pygame.Rect class to handle rectangular collisions:

```python
Copy code
rect1 = pygame.Rect(50, 50, 100, 100)
rect2 = pygame.Rect(100, 100, 100, 100)

if rect1.colliderect(rect2):
    # Handle collision
```

2. Handling Complex Collisions

Circular Collisions

For circular objects, use distance calculations:

```python
Copy code
import math

def collide_circle(circle1, circle2):
```

45

```
distance = math.sqrt((circle1[0] - circle2[0])**2 +
(circle1[1] - circle2[1])**2)
return distance < (circle1[2] + circle2[2])
```

Pixel-Perfect Collisions

For precise collisions, use pixel masks:

```python
Copy code
def collide_mask(sprite1, sprite2):
    return pygame.sprite.collide_mask(sprite1, sprite2)
```

3. Implementing Basic Physics

Basic physics involve simulating movement and interactions between objects based on forces, velocities, and collisions.

Gravity and Movement

Simulate gravity and movement with basic physics equations:

```python
Copy code
class PhysicsSprite(pygame.sprite.Sprite):
    def __init__(self):
        super().__init__()
        self.image = pygame.Surface((50, 50))
        self.image.fill((255, 0, 0))
        self.rect = self.image.get_rect()
        self.rect.center = (400, 300)
        self.velocity = pygame.Vector2(0, 0)
        self.gravity = 0.5

    def update(self):
        self.velocity.y += self.gravity
        self.rect.x += self.velocity.x
        self.rect.y += self.velocity.y
```

4. Advanced Physics Techniques
Collision Response

Implement responses to collisions, such as bouncing or stopping:

```python
Copy code
def handle_collision(sprite, wall):
    if sprite.rect.colliderect(wall.rect):
        sprite.velocity.x = -sprite.velocity.x  # Bounce off wall
```

Physics Libraries

For more advanced physics simulations, consider using external libraries such as Pygame's pymunk or Box2D.

Summary

In this chapter, you've explored advanced techniques in Pygame, including sound and music integration, animations and sprite management, and collision detection and physics. By mastering these techniques, you can create more dynamic, interactive, and polished games. Continue experimenting with these concepts and exploring new techniques to enhance your game development skills and create engaging gaming experiences.

6. Introduction to Arcade

A rcade is a modern Python library designed for creating 2D games with ease and efficiency. It offers a user-friendly interface and powerful features, making it an excellent choice for both beginners and experienced developers. This chapter will provide a comprehensive overview of Arcade, including its installation, project setup, and key concepts such as sprites, views, and input handling.

Arcade Overview and Installation

1. Overview of Arcade

Arcade is a Python library that simplifies the process of creating 2D games by providing a high-level API for managing graphics, sound, and user input. It is built on top of OpenGL and Pyglet, offering enhanced performance and capabilities compared to some other game development libraries. Arcade's design emphasizes ease of use and flexibility, making it accessible for both new and experienced developers.

Key Features:

- **Easy to Learn:** Arcade has a straightforward API and comprehensive documentation, making it easy to get started with game development.
- **Modern Graphics:** Utilizes OpenGL for high-performance graphics rendering.
- **Flexible:** Supports various game mechanics, including sprites, animations, and physics.

- **Active Community:** Benefits from an active community and regular updates.

2. Installing Arcade

To get started with Arcade, you need to install it using pip, the Python package installer. You can install Arcade with the following command:

```bash
Copy code
pip install arcade
```

3. Verifying Installation

After installation, verify that Arcade is installed correctly by running a simple script that initializes a window:

```python
Copy code
import arcade

def main():
    arcade.open_window(600, 400, "Arcade Installation Test")
    arcade.set_background_color(arcade.color.WHITE)
    arcade.start_render()
    arcade.finish_render()
    arcade.run()

if __name__ == "__main__":
    main()
```

If the script runs without errors and you see a white window, Arcade is installed correctly.

Setting Up an Arcade Project

1. Creating a Basic Project Structure

When starting a new Arcade project, it's helpful to organize your files and directories for better management. A typical project structure might look like this:

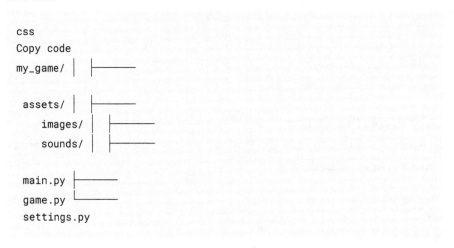

```css
Copy code
my_game/ | ├──────
    assets/ | ├──────
        images/ | ├──────
        sounds/ | ├──────

    main.py ├──────
    game.py └──────
    settings.py
```

- **assets/:** Directory for storing game assets like images and sounds.
- **main.py:** Entry point of the game, responsible for initializing the game window.
- **game.py:** Contains the main game logic and game state.
- **settings.py:** Configuration file for game settings and constants.

2. Writing the Main Game Script

The main.py script is the entry point of the game. It initializes the game window and starts the game loop. Here's a simple example:

```python
Copy code
import arcade
from game import Game
```

```python
def main():
    arcade.open_window(800, 600, "My Arcade Game")
    arcade.set_background_color(arcade.color.ASK_BLUE)

    game = Game()
    arcade.schedule(game.update, 1/60)   # Update game 60 times per
    second

    arcade.run()

if __name__ == "__main__":
    main()
```

3. Creating the Game Logic

In the game.py file, you define the Game class that handles game logic,
including updating game state and rendering:

```python
python
Copy code
import arcade

class Game(arcade.Window):
    def __init__(self):
        super().__init__(800, 600, "My Arcade Game")
        self.set_update_rate(1/60)   # Set the update rate to 60 FPS

        # Initialize game variables
        self.player_sprite =
        arcade.Sprite("assets/images/player.png", scale=0.5)
        self.player_sprite.center_x = 400
        self.player_sprite.center_y = 300

    def on_draw(self):
        arcade.start_render()
        self.player_sprite.draw()

    def update(self, delta_time):
```

```
        # Update game state here
        pass

    def on_key_press(self, key, modifiers):
        # Handle key press events
        pass

    def on_key_release(self, key, modifiers):
        # Handle key release events
        pass
```

4. Configuring Settings

The settings.py file is used to store game constants and configuration settings:

```python
Copy code
# settings.py

WINDOW_WIDTH = 800
WINDOW_HEIGHT = 600
WINDOW_TITLE = "My Arcade Game"
```

You can import these settings into your main game script or game logic as needed:

```python
Copy code
import settings

arcade.open_window(settings.WINDOW_WIDTH, settings.WINDOW_HEIGHT,
settings.WINDOW_TITLE)
```

Basic Arcade Concepts: Sprites, Views, and Input

1. Sprites

Sprites are the visual elements of your game. In Arcade, sprites are managed using the arcade.Sprite class, which provides functionality for rendering and moving objects.

Creating Sprites

To create a sprite, you need an image file and the arcade.Sprite class:

```python
Copy code
player_sprite = arcade.Sprite("assets/images/player.png",
scale=0.5)
player_sprite.center_x = 400
player_sprite.center_y = 300
```

Sprite Methods

- **draw():** Renders the sprite on the screen.
- **update():** Updates the sprite's position and state.
- **change_x and change_y:** Control sprite movement.

Handling Sprite Movement

Update the sprite's position by modifying its change_x and change_y attributes:

```python
Copy code
def update(self, delta_time):
    self.player_sprite.center_x += self.player_sprite.change_x
    self.player_sprite.center_y += self.player_sprite.change_y
```

2. Views

Views are used to manage different sections of the game, such as menus, gameplay, and game over screens. Arcade provides the arcade.View class for this purpose.

Creating a View

Subclass arcade.View and override its methods:

```python
Copy code
import arcade

class MainMenuView(arcade.View):
    def __init__(self):
        super().__init__()

    def on_draw(self):
        arcade.start_render()
        arcade.draw_text("Main Menu", 400, 300,
        arcade.color.WHITE, 50)

    def on_key_press(self, key, modifiers):
        if key == arcade.key.ENTER:
            game_view = GameView()
            self.window.show_view(game_view)
```

Switching Views

To switch views, use the window.show_view() method:

```python
Copy code
main_menu_view = MainMenuView()
window.show_view(main_menu_view)
```

3. Input Handling

Arcade provides methods to handle keyboard and mouse input.

Keyboard Input

Override the on_key_press and on_key_release methods to handle key events:

```python
Copy code
def on_key_press(self, key, modifiers):
    if key == arcade.key.LEFT:
        self.player_sprite.change_x = -5
    elif key == arcade.key.RIGHT:
        self.player_sprite.change_x = 5

def on_key_release(self, key, modifiers):
    if key in (arcade.key.LEFT, arcade.key.RIGHT):
        self.player_sprite.change_x = 0
```

Mouse Input

Handle mouse events using on_mouse_press, on_mouse_release, and on_mouse_motion:

```python
Copy code
def on_mouse_press(self, x, y, button, modifiers):
    print(f"Mouse clicked at ({x}, {y})")
```

4. Input and Sprite Interaction

Combine input handling with sprite interactions to create dynamic gameplay:

```python
Copy code
def on_key_press(self, key, modifiers):
    if key == arcade.key.SPACE:
        self.player_sprite.change_y = 10  # Make the player jump

def update(self, delta_time):
    self.player_sprite.center_y += self.player_sprite.change_y
    # Implement gravity
    self.player_sprite.change_y -= 1
```

Advanced Techniques and Best Practices

1. Managing Multiple Sprites

For games with many sprites, use arcade.SpriteList to manage and update groups of sprites efficiently:

```python
Copy code
class Game(arcade.Window):
    def __init__(self):
        super().__init__(800, 600, "My Arcade Game")
        self.all_sprites = arcade.SpriteList()
        self.player_sprite =
        arcade.Sprite("assets/images/player.png", scale=0.5)
        self.all_sprites.append(self.player_sprite)

    def on_draw(self):
        arcade.start_render()
        self.all_sprites.draw()

    def update(self, delta_time):
        self.all_sprites.update()
```

2. Using Particles for Effects

Particles can enhance your game with effects like explosions or sparks. Create a particle system by defining a Particle class and managing particles in a list:

```python
Copy code
class Particle(arcade.Sprite):
    def __init__(self, x, y):
        super().__init__("assets/images/particle.png")
        self.center_x = x
        self.center_y = y
        self.change_x = random.uniform(-2, 2)
        self.change_y = random.uniform(-2, 2)
```

```
    self.life = 100

def update(self):
    self.center_x += self.change_x
    self.center_y += self.change_y
    self.life -= 1
    if self.life <= 0:
        self.remove_from_sprite_lists()
```

3. Optimizing Performance

Optimize game performance by minimizing expensive operations and using efficient data structures:

- **Batch Drawing:** Use arcade.SpriteList to batch draw operations.
- **Optimize Sprites:** Use SpriteSheet for animations and reduce the number of draw calls.
- **Efficient Updates:** Minimize work done in the update() method to ensure smooth gameplay.

Summary

In this chapter, you've learned about the Arcade library, including its installation, project setup, and key concepts such as sprites, views, and input handling. Arcade's simplicity and power make it an excellent choice for creating 2D games, and by understanding these core concepts, you'll be well-equipped to develop engaging and polished games. Continue exploring Arcade's features and experimenting with advanced techniques to enhance your game development skills.

7. Developing Games with Arcade

rcade is a robust library for developing 2D games in Python. This chapter delves into practical game development using Arcade, covering the creation of a simple game, exploring advanced features like physics engines and tilemaps, and customizing and extending Arcade for specific needs. By the end of this chapter, you'll be equipped with the skills to build more sophisticated and engaging games.

Creating a Simple Game with Arcade

1. Conceptualizing the Game

Before diving into code, outline your game's concept. For this example, we'll create a basic "Catch the Falling Objects" game where the player controls a basket to catch falling objects and score points.

2. Setting Up the Project

Create a project directory with the following structure:

```css
Copy code
catch_the_falls/ |  |————

  assets/ |  |————
     images/ | |  |————
        basket.png | |   |————
        falling_object.png |  |————
```

```
sounds/  |  └─────
 music/  |  ├─────

main.py  └─────
game.py
```

3. Implementing the Game Logic

3.1. Game Initialization

In main.py, initialize the Arcade window and set up the game loop:

```python
Copy code
import arcade
from game import Game

def main():
    arcade.open_window(800, 600, "Catch the Falling Objects")
    arcade.set_background_color(arcade.color.ASK_BLUE)

    game = Game()
    arcade.schedule(game.update, 1/60)  # Update game 60 times per
    second

    arcade.run()

if __name__ == "__main__":
    main()
```

3.2. Game Class

In game.py, define the Game class, which handles game initialization, updates, and rendering:

```python
Copy code
import arcade
import random
```

```python
class Game(arcade.Window):
    def __init__(self):
        super().__init__(800, 600, "Catch the Falling Objects")
        arcade.set_background_color(arcade.color.ASK_BLUE)

        # Load images
        self.basket = arcade.Sprite("assets/images/basket.png",
        scale=0.5)
        self.basket.center_x = self.width // 2
        self.basket.center_y = 50

        self.falling_objects = arcade.SpriteList()
        self.score = 0

        # Set up the player controls
        self.player_speed = 5

    def on_draw(self):
        arcade.start_render()
        self.basket.draw()
        self.falling_objects.draw()
        # Draw the score
        score_text = f"Score: {self.score}"
        arcade.draw_text(score_text, 10, self.height - 20,
        arcade.color.WHITE, 14)

    def update(self, delta_time):
        # Move basket with keyboard input
        keys = arcade.key.get_pressed()
        if keys[arcade.key.LEFT]:
            self.basket.center_x -= self.player_speed
        if keys[arcade.key.RIGHT]:
            self.basket.center_x += self.player_speed

        # Keep basket within screen bounds
        if self.basket.left < 0:
            self.basket.left = 0
        if self.basket.right > self.width:
            self.basket.right = self.width
```

```python
    # Add new falling objects
    if random.random() < 0.02:
        falling_object =
        arcade.Sprite("assets/images/falling_object.png",
        scale=0.5)
        falling_object.center_x = random.randint(0, self.width)
        falling_object.center_y = self.height
        falling_object.change_y = -5
        self.falling_objects.append(falling_object)

    # Update falling objects
    self.falling_objects.update()

    # Check for collisions
    for obj in self.falling_objects:
        if obj.bottom < 0:
            obj.remove_from_sprite_lists()
        if obj.collides_with_sprite(self.basket):
            obj.remove_from_sprite_lists()
            self.score += 1
```

3.3. Adding Input Handling

In the Game class, handle player input for moving the basket:

```python
python
Copy code
def on_key_press(self, key, modifiers):
    if key == arcade.key.LEFT:
        self.basket.change_x = -self.player_speed
    elif key == arcade.key.RIGHT:
        self.basket.change_x = self.player_speed

def on_key_release(self, key, modifiers):
    if key in (arcade.key.LEFT, arcade.key.RIGHT):
        self.basket.change_x = 0
```

Advanced Features: Physics Engine and Tilemaps

1. Using the Physics Engine

Arcade integrates with the pybullet physics engine for handling complex physics simulations. However, Arcade also provides basic physics functionality suitable for many 2D games.

1.1. Integrating Physics

To use basic physics, you can implement gravity, collision responses, and velocity changes:

```python
Copy code
class PhysicsSprite(arcade.Sprite):
    def __init__(self, image, scale=1):
        super().__init__(image, scale)
        self.change_x = 0
        self.change_y = 0
        self.gravity = -0.5  # Gravity force

    def update(self):
        self.change_y += self.gravity
        self.center_x += self.change_x
        self.center_y += self.change_y
```

1.2. Applying Physics to Game Objects

In the Game class, use the PhysicsSprite class for falling objects:

```python
Copy code
class Game(arcade.Window):
    def __init__(self):
        super().__init__(800, 600, "Catch the Falling Objects")
        self.basket = arcade.Sprite("assets/images/basket.png",
        scale=0.5)
        self.basket.center_x = self.width // 2
        self.basket.center_y = 50
```

```python
        self.falling_objects = arcade.SpriteList()
        self.score = 0

    def update(self, delta_time):
        keys = arcade.key.get_pressed()
        if keys[arcade.key.LEFT]:
            self.basket.center_x -= 5
        if keys[arcade.key.RIGHT]:
            self.basket.center_x += 5

        if self.basket.left < 0:
            self.basket.left = 0
        if self.basket.right > self.width:
            self.basket.right = self.width

        if random.random() < 0.02:
            falling_object =
            PhysicsSprite("assets/images/falling_object.png",
            scale=0.5)
            falling_object.center_x = random.randint(0, self.width)
            falling_object.center_y = self.height
            falling_object.change_y = -5
            self.falling_objects.append(falling_object)

        self.falling_objects.update()

        for obj in self.falling_objects:
            if obj.bottom < 0:
                obj.remove_from_sprite_lists()
            if obj.collides_with_sprite(self.basket):
                obj.remove_from_sprite_lists()
                self.score += 1
```

2. Using Tilemaps

Tilemaps are used to create game levels with a grid of tiles. Arcade supports tilemaps through the arcade.Tilemap class, which allows for efficient level design.

2.1. Creating a Tilemap

First, create a tilemap using a tool like Tiled Map Editor, then export it as a

.json file. For this example, assume you have a tilemap file level.json and a tileset image tiles.png.

2.2. Loading and Rendering Tilemaps

In the Game class, load and render the tilemap:

```python
Copy code
import arcade

class Game(arcade.Window):
    def __init__(self):
        super().__init__(800, 600, "Tilemap Example")
        self.tilemap = arcade.tilemap.read_tmx("assets/level.json")

    def on_draw(self):
        arcade.start_render()
        self.tilemap.draw()
```

2.3. Adding Tilemap Interactions

For interactive tilemaps, you may need to handle tile collisions or use tile properties to define interactive elements:

```python
Copy code
class Game(arcade.Window):
    def __init__(self):
        super().__init__(800, 600, "Tilemap Example")
        self.tilemap = arcade.tilemap.read_tmx("assets/level.json")
        self.player = arcade.Sprite("assets/images/player.png",
        scale=0.5)
        self.player.center_x = 400
        self.player.center_y = 300

    def update(self, delta_time):
        self.player.update()

        # Check for collisions with tiles
```

```
        if self.tilemap.layer_names:
            for tile in self.tilemap.layers['collision']:
                if self.player.collides_with_sprite(tile):
                    # Handle collision
                    pass

    def on_draw(self):
        arcade.start_render()
        self.tilemap.draw()
        self.player.draw()
```

Customizing and Extending Arcade

1. Customizing Arcade

Arcade provides a high degree of customization for game development. You can customize the game loop, rendering, and user interface to fit your needs.

1.1. Customizing the Game Loop

Override the on_update() method to control how frequently the game state updates:

```python
Copy code
class CustomGame(arcade.Window):
    def __init__(self):
        super().__init__(800, 600, "Custom Game Loop")
        arcade.schedule(self.update, 1/30)  # Update 30 times per
        second

    def update(self, delta_time):
        # Custom update logic
        pass
```

1.2. Customizing Rendering

Override the on_draw() method to customize rendering behavior:

```python
Copy code
def on_draw(self):
    arcade.start_render()
    # Custom rendering logic
    self.background_color = arcade.color.BLACK
    arcade.draw_text("Welcome to My Game", self.width // 2,
    self.height // 2, arcade.color.WHITE, 24, anchor_x="center",
    anchor_y="center")
```

2. Extending Arcade

To extend Arcade, you can create custom classes or integrate external libraries.

2.1. Creating Custom Sprites

Create a custom sprite class by subclassing arcade.Sprite:

```python
Copy code
class CustomSprite(arcade.Sprite):
    def __init__(self, image, scale=1):
        super().__init__(image, scale)
        self.custom_property = 0

    def custom_method(self):
        # Custom behavior
        pass
```

2.2. Integrating External Libraries

Integrate external libraries like numpy for complex calculations or pygame for additional functionality:

```python
Copy code
import numpy as np
```

```
class GameWithNumpy(arcade.Window):
    def __init__(self):
        super().__init__(800, 600, "Game with Numpy")

    def update(self, delta_time):
        # Use numpy for calculations
        data = np.array([1, 2, 3])
        result = np.mean(data)
        print(result)
```

Summary

In this chapter, you've explored developing games with Arcade, starting from creating a simple game, incorporating advanced features like physics engines and tilemaps, to customizing and extending Arcade. By mastering these techniques, you can build sophisticated and engaging games while leveraging Arcade's powerful capabilities. Continue experimenting and exploring new features to enhance your game development skills and create memorable gaming experience.

8. Introduction to Panda3D

Panda3D is a powerful and versatile 3D game engine developed by Disney and maintained by the community. It provides a robust framework for creating immersive 3D games and simulations, making it a popular choice for developers looking to delve into 3D graphics and complex interactions. This chapter introduces Panda3D, including its installation, project setup, and fundamental concepts like scene graphs and rendering.

Panda3D Overview and Installation

1. Overview of Panda3D

Panda3D is a comprehensive open-source 3D game engine that supports both Python and C++. It is designed for creating high-quality 3D applications and games with features such as real-time rendering, physics simulation, and advanced graphics effects. Panda3D is used in various industries, from entertainment to education, due to its flexibility and ease of use.

Key Features:

- **Real-time Rendering:** Supports advanced rendering techniques such as shaders, dynamic lighting, and shadows.
- **Scene Graph System:** Utilizes a hierarchical scene graph for managing and rendering complex 3D environments.
- **Physics Engine:** Integrated support for physical simulations, including collision detection and response.

- **Animation System:** Robust tools for animating characters and objects.
- **Cross-Platform:** Works on Windows, macOS, and Linux.

2. Installing Panda3D

To get started with Panda3D, you need to install it via pip, the Python package manager. Ensure that you have Python 3.6 or newer installed before proceeding.

2.1. Installing via Pip

Open a terminal or command prompt and run the following command:

```bash
Copy code
pip install panda3d
```

This command installs the latest version of Panda3D and its dependencies.

2.2. Verifying Installation

After installation, verify that Panda3D is correctly installed by running a simple script that initializes a window and renders a basic scene:

```python
Copy code
from panda3d.core import Point3
from direct.showbase.ShowBase import ShowBase

class MyApp(ShowBase):
    def __init__(self):
        ShowBase.__init__(self)
        self.add_model()

    def add_model(self):
        self.environ = self.loader.load_model("models/environment")
        self.environ.reparent_to(self.render)
        self.environ.set_scale(0.25, 0.25, 0.25)
        self.environ.set_pos(-8, 42, 0)
```

```
app = MyApp()
app.run()
```

If the script runs without errors and you see a 3D environment in the window, Panda3D is successfully installed.

Setting Up a Panda3D Project

1. Creating a Project Directory

Organizing your Panda3D project files is crucial for maintainability. A typical project structure might look like this:

```
arduino
Copy code
my_panda3d_game/

  assets/
    models/
    textures/
    sounds/

  main.py
  game.py
  config.py
```

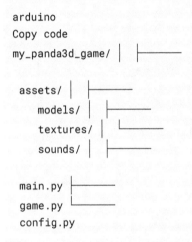

- **assets/:** Directory for storing game assets like models, textures, and sounds.
- **main.py:** Entry point of the game, responsible for initializing the application.
- **game.py:** Contains the main game logic and state management.
- **config.py:** Configuration file for game settings and constants.

2. Writing the Main Application Script

The main.py script initializes the Panda3D application and starts the game loop. Here's an example:

```python
Copy code
from panda3d.core import Point3
from direct.showbase.ShowBase import ShowBase
from game import Game

def main():
    app = Game()
    app.run()

if __name__ == "__main__":
    main()
```

3. Defining the Game Class

In game.py, define the Game class that handles game initialization, updates, and rendering:

```python
Copy code
from panda3d.core import LVector3f
from direct.showbase.ShowBase import ShowBase

class Game(ShowBase):
    def __init__(self):
        ShowBase.__init__(self)
        self.setup_scene()

    def setup_scene(self):
        self.environ = self.loader.load_model("models/environment")
        self.environ.reparent_to(self.render)
        self.environ.set_scale(0.25, 0.25, 0.25)
        self.environ.set_pos(-8, 42, 0)
        self.environ.set_color(1, 1, 1, 1)

    def update(self, task):
```

```
    # Update game logic here
    return task.cont
```

4. Configuring Settings

The config.py file is used to store game constants and settings:

```python
Copy code
# config.py

WINDOW_WIDTH = 800
WINDOW_HEIGHT = 600
WINDOW_TITLE = "My Panda3D Game"
```

Import and use these settings in your main script:

```python
Copy code
from config import WINDOW_WIDTH, WINDOW_HEIGHT, WINDOW_TITLE

class Game(ShowBase):
    def __init__(self):
        ShowBase.__init__(self)
        self.win.set_size(WINDOW_WIDTH, WINDOW_HEIGHT)
        self.win.set_title(WINDOW_TITLE)
        self.setup_scene()
```

Basic Panda3D Concepts: Scene Graphs and Rendering

1. Scene Graphs

Panda3D uses a scene graph to manage and organize 3D objects. The scene graph is a hierarchical structure where each node represents an object or a group of objects. Nodes can have children, allowing for complex hierarchies and transformations.

1.1. Node Types

- **NodePath:** The fundamental class used to manage nodes in the scene graph. It represents an object in the scene and can be manipulated to control its position, orientation, and scale.
- **ModelNode:** Represents 3D models in the scene. It can be loaded from various file formats and manipulated within the scene graph.
- **LightNode:** Represents lights in the scene. Different types of lights (e.g., point lights, directional lights) can be added to illuminate objects.

1.2. Working with Nodes

Create and manipulate nodes using the NodePath class:

```python
Copy code
from panda3d.core import NodePath

class Game(ShowBase):
    def __init__(self):
        ShowBase.__init__(self)
        self.create_objects()

    def create_objects(self):
        # Create a node for the environment
        self.environ = NodePath("Environment")
        self.environ.reparent_to(self.render)
        self.environ.set_pos(0, 0, 0)
```

2. Rendering in Panda3D

Rendering in Panda3D involves displaying the contents of the scene graph on the screen. Panda3D's rendering process includes loading assets, setting up cameras, and rendering frames.

2.1. Loading Models

Load 3D models into the scene using the loader:

```python
Copy code
```

73

```
class Game(ShowBase):
    def __init__(self):
        ShowBase.__init__(self)
        self.load_model()

    def load_model(self):
        self.model = self.loader.load_model("models/my_model")
        self.model.reparent_to(self.render)
        self.model.set_scale(0.5, 0.5, 0.5)
        self.model.set_pos(0, 10, 0)
```

2.2. Setting Up the Camera

Configure the camera to view the scene from different angles:

```python
Copy code
class Game(ShowBase):
    def __init__(self):
        ShowBase.__init__(self)
        self.setup_camera()

    def setup_camera(self):
        self.camera.set_pos(0, -20, 3)
        self.camera.look_at(0, 0, 0)
```

2.3. Rendering Frames

Panda3D automatically handles rendering frames at a consistent frame rate. You can override the task function to perform custom updates:

```python
Copy code
class Game(ShowBase):
    def __init__(self):
        ShowBase.__init__(self)
        self.taskMgr.add(self.update, "update")
```

```
def update(self, task):
    # Update logic
    return task.cont
```

2.4. Handling Lights and Shadows

Add lights to illuminate the scene and cast shadows:

```python
Copy code
from panda3d.core import PointLight, AmbientLight

class Game(ShowBase):
    def __init__(self):
        ShowBase.__init__(self)
        self.setup_lights()

    def setup_lights(self):
        ambient_light = AmbientLight("ambient_light")
        ambient_light.set_color((0.2, 0.2, 0.2, 1))
        ambient_light_np =
        self.render.attach_new_node(ambient_light)
        self.render.set_light(ambient_light_np)

        point_light = PointLight("point_light")
        point_light.set_color((1, 1, 1, 1))
        point_light_np = self.render.attach_new_node(point_light)
        point_light_np.set_pos(10, -10, 10)
        self.render.set_light(point_light_np)
```

Summary

In this chapter, you've explored the basics of Panda3D, including its installation, project setup, and fundamental concepts like scene graphs and rendering. Panda3D's powerful features and flexible architecture make it an excellent choice for creating complex 3D games and simulations. By understanding these core concepts, you're well on your way to developing engaging 3D applications and taking full advantage of Panda3D's capabilities. Continue experimenting with Panda3D's features and exploring advanced topics to further enhance your game development skills.

9. Creating 3D Games with Panda3D

Creating 3D games with Panda3D involves a deep understanding of 3D concepts and how to apply them within the engine. This chapter will guide you through building a basic 3D game, handling 3D models and textures, and implementing camera controls and lighting. By the end of this chapter, you will be equipped to create engaging 3D experiences using Panda3D.

Building a Basic 3D Game

1. Conceptualizing the Game

Before you start coding, outline the concept of your 3D game. For this example, we'll create a simple "3D Maze Runner" game where the player navigates a maze and collects items.

2. Project Setup

Create a directory structure for your Panda3D project:

```
arduino
Copy code
maze_runner/ │ ├──────

  assets/ │ ├─────
    models/ │ ├─────
    textures/ │ └─────
    sounds/ │ ├─────
```

```
main.py  ├──────
game.py  └──────
config.py
```

3. Implementing the Game Logic

3.1. Main Application Script

In main.py, set up the Panda3D window and initialize the game:

```python
Copy code
from panda3d.core import Point3
from direct.showbase.ShowBase import ShowBase
from game import Game

def main():
    app = Game()
    app.run()

if __name__ == "__main__":
    main()
```

3.2. Game Class Implementation

In game.py, define the Game class that handles game initialization, updates, and rendering:

```python
Copy code
from panda3d.core import LVector3f, AmbientLight, DirectionalLight
from direct.showbase.ShowBase import ShowBase

class Game(ShowBase):
    def __init__(self):
        ShowBase.__init__(self)
        self.setup_scene()
        self.setup_lights()
```

```
    self.setup_camera()
    self.taskMgr.add(self.update, "update")

def setup_scene(self):
    # Load maze model and setup environment
    self.maze = self.loader.load_model("models/maze")
    self.maze.reparent_to(self.render)
    self.maze.set_scale(1, 1, 1)
    self.maze.set_pos(0, 0, 0)

    # Load player model
    self.player = self.loader.load_model("models/player")
    self.player.reparent_to(self.render)
    self.player.set_scale(0.5, 0.5, 0.5)
    self.player.set_pos(0, 0, 1)

    # Add collision detection
    self.collision_handler = self.collision_traverser =
    CollisionTraverser()
    self.collision_queue = CollisionHandlerQueue()

    self.player_collision_node =
    self.player.attach_new_node(CollisionNode('player'))
    self.player_collision_node.node().add_solid(CollisionSphere(0,
    0, 0, 1))

    self.collision_traverser.add_collider(self.player_collision_node,
    self.collision_queue)

def setup_lights(self):
    ambient_light = AmbientLight("ambient_light")
    ambient_light.set_color((0.5, 0.5, 0.5, 1))
    ambient_light_np =
    self.render.attach_new_node(ambient_light)
    self.render.set_light(ambient_light_np)

    directional_light = DirectionalLight("directional_light")
    directional_light.set_color((1, 1, 1, 1))
    directional_light_np =
    self.render.attach_new_node(directional_light)
```

```
        directional_light_np.look_at(LVector3f(-1, -1, -1))
        self.render.set_light(directional_light_np)

    def setup_camera(self):
        self.camera.set_pos(0, -10, 5)
        self.camera.look_at(0, 0, 0)

    def update(self, task):
        # Update game logic here
        return task.cont
```

4. Handling 3D Models and Textures

4.1. Loading 3D Models

Panda3D supports various model formats, including .egg, .bam, and .obj. Use the loader to load models:

```python
Copy code
class Game(ShowBase):
    def setup_scene(self):
        self.maze = self.loader.load_model("models/maze.bam")
        self.player = self.loader.load_model("models/player.egg")
```

4.2. Applying Textures

Load and apply textures to your models:

```python
Copy code
class Game(ShowBase):
    def setup_scene(self):
        self.maze = self.loader.load_model
("models/maze.bam")
        self.maze.set_texture
(self.loader.load_texture
("textures/maze_texture.jpg"))
```

```
        self.player = self.loader.
load_model("models/player.egg")
        self.player.set_texture
(self.loader.load_texture
("textures/player_texture.jpg"))
```

4.3. UV Mapping

Ensure your 3D models have proper UV mapping to correctly display textures. Use tools like Blender to map textures to your models.

5. Implementing Camera Controls and Lighting

5.1. Camera Controls

Implement camera controls to navigate the scene:

```python
python
Copy code
from panda3d.core import Point3

class Game(ShowBase):
    def __init__(self):
        ShowBase.__init__(self)
        self.setup_camera()
        self.camera_speed = 10

    def setup_camera(self):
        self.camera.set_pos(0, -10, 5)
        self.camera.look_at(0, 0, 0)

    def update(self, task):
        if self.mouseWatcherNode.has_mouse():
            mouse_x = self.mouseWatcherNode.get_mouse_x()
            mouse_y = self.mouseWatcherNode.get_mouse_y()
            self.camera.look_at(mouse_x, mouse_y, 0)
        return task.cont
```

5.2. Advanced Camera Controls

For more advanced camera controls, you can implement first-person or third-person perspectives:

```python
Copy code
from panda3d.core import LVector3f, NodePath

class Game(ShowBase):
    def __init__(self):
        ShowBase.__init__(self)
        self.camera_speed = 10

    def update(self, task):
        # First-person movement controls
        if self.mouseWatcherNode.has_mouse():
            if
            self.mouseWatcherNode.is_button_down(MouseButton.right()):
                self.camera.set_y(self.camera, self.camera_speed *
                self.mouseWatcherNode.get_mouse_y())
                self.camera.set_x(self.camera, self.camera_speed *
                self.mouseWatcherNode.get_mouse_x())
        return task.cont
```

5.3. Lighting

Experiment with different types of lights to create mood and atmosphere:

```python
Copy code
from panda3d.core import PointLight, DirectionalLight, AmbientLight

class Game(ShowBase):
    def setup_lights(self):
        ambient_light = AmbientLight("ambient_light")
        ambient_light.set_color((0.5, 0.5, 0.5, 1))
        ambient_light_np =
        self.render.attach_new_node(ambient_light)
        self.render.set_light(ambient_light_np)

        directional_light = DirectionalLight("directional_light")
        directional_light.set_color((1, 1, 1, 1))
```

```
directional_light_np =
self.render.attach_new_node(directional_light)
directional_light_np.look_at(LVector3f(-1, -1, -1))
self.render.set_light(directional_light_np)

point_light = PointLight("point_light")
point_light.set_color((1, 1, 1, 1))
point_light_np = self.render.attach_new_node(point_light)
point_light_np.set_pos(10, 10, 10)
self.render.set_light(point_light_np)
```

Summary

In this chapter, you've learned how to create a basic 3D game with Panda3D, handle 3D models and textures, and implement camera controls and lighting. Panda3D's powerful features allow you to develop complex and visually appealing 3D games. By mastering these concepts, you can create engaging 3D experiences and push the boundaries of your game development skills. Continue experimenting with Panda3D's advanced features and integrating new techniques to further enhance your game development projects.

10. Advanced Panda3D Techniques

As you delve deeper into game development with Panda3D, mastering advanced techniques will enhance your ability to create sophisticated and engaging 3D games. This chapter explores three crucial advanced topics: animation and rigging, physics and collision detection, and integrating AI and pathfinding. Each section will provide practical insights and examples to help you leverage Panda3D's capabilities effectively.

Animation and Rigging

1. Understanding Animation in Panda3D

Animation in Panda3D allows you to bring characters and objects to life. Panda3D supports various types of animation, including skeletal animation, vertex animation, and procedural animation.

1.1. Skeletal Animation

Skeletal animation is the most common method for animating characters. It involves creating a skeleton (or rig) and then binding a mesh to this skeleton. The mesh deforms according to the movements of the skeleton.

Creating and Importing Skeletal Animations

Use 3D modeling tools like Blender to create skeletal animations. Export your model and animation in a format supported by Panda3D, such as .egg or .bam. Here's an example of how to load and play an animation:

```python
Copy code
from panda3d.core import Point3
from direct.showbase.ShowBase import ShowBase

class Game(ShowBase):
    def __init__(self):
        ShowBase.__init__(self)
        self.setup_animation()

    def setup_animation(self):
        # Load the model with animations
        self.character =
        self.loader.load_model("models/character.bam")
        self.character.reparent_to(self.render)
        self.character.set_scale(0.5, 0.5, 0.5)
        self.character.set_pos(0, 0, 0)

        # Loop through available animations
        self.character.loop("walk")
        # Or play a specific animation once
        # self.character.play("run")

app = Game()
app.run()
```

1.2. Rigging

Rigging involves creating a skeleton with bones and assigning weights to vertices of the mesh so that it deforms correctly when the bones move. Ensure that the rig is properly set up in your modeling software.

Animating Characters

In Panda3D, use the AnimationPool and Animation classes to control animations. For complex animations, you may need to create and manage multiple animations within a single character model.

```python
Copy code
```

```
from panda3d.core import AnimationPool, Animation

class Game(ShowBase):
    def setup_animation(self):
        self.character =
        self.loader.load_model("models/character.bam")
        self.character.reparent_to(self.render)

        # Load animations
        self.animations = AnimationPool(self.character)
        self.animations.load("walk", "models/character_walk.bam")
        self.animations.load("run", "models/character_run.bam")

        # Play animations
        self.character.loop("walk")

app = Game()
app.run()
```

Physics and Collision Detection

1. Introduction to Physics in Panda3D

Physics simulation adds realism to your game by simulating real-world physical interactions. Panda3D integrates physics engines for handling complex interactions, including gravity, collisions, and object dynamics.

1.1. Basic Physics Setup

Panda3D provides a basic physics simulation environment through its Bullet physics engine. To use Bullet, you need to set up the physics world and add physics nodes to your objects.

Setting Up Bullet Physics

Install the Bullet physics engine and set up the basic physics world in your game:

```python
Copy code
from panda3d.bullet import BulletWorld, BulletBoxShape,
BulletRigidBodyNode
from panda3d.core import Vec3

class Game(ShowBase):
    def __init__(self):
        ShowBase.__init__(self)
        self.setup_physics()

    def setup_physics(self):
        # Create Bullet world
        self.physics_world = BulletWorld()

        # Create a ground plane
        ground_shape = BulletBoxShape(Vec3(50, 50, 1))
        ground_node = BulletRigidBodyNode('ground')
        ground_node.add_shape(ground_shape)
        ground_np = self.render.attach_new_node(ground_node)
        self.physics_world.attach(ground_node)
        self.physics_world.set_gravity(Vec3(0, 0, -9.8))

        # Create a dynamic object
        box_shape = BulletBoxShape(Vec3(1, 1, 1))
        box_node = BulletRigidBodyNode('box')
        box_node.set_mass(1)
        box_node.add_shape(box_shape)
        box_np = self.render.attach_new_node(box_node)
        self.physics_world.attach(box_node)
        box_np.set_pos(0, 0, 10)

    def update(self, task):
        self.physics_world.do_physics(globalClock.get_dt())
        return task.cont

app = Game()
app.run()
```

1.2. Collision Detection

Collision detection is crucial for interactions between game objects. Panda3D's collision system allows you to set up collision solids and detect collisions.

Setting Up Collisions

Define collision solids and add collision handlers:

```python
Copy code
from panda3d.core import CollisionSphere, CollisionNode
from panda3d.bullet import BulletBoxShape, BulletRigidBodyNode,
BulletWorld

class Game(ShowBase):
    def setup_collisions(self):
        # Create collision node for player
        self.player_collision_node = CollisionNode('player')
        self.player_collision_node.add_solid(CollisionSphere(0, 0,
        0, 1))
        self.player_collision_np =
        self.render.attach_new_node(self.player_collision_node)

        # Create collision handler
        self.collision_handler = CollisionHandlerQueue()
        self.collision_traverser = CollisionTraverser()
        self.collision_traverser.add_collider(self.player_collision_np,
        self.collision_handler)

    def update(self, task):
        self.collision_traverser.traverse(self.render)
        if self.collision_handler.get_num_entries() > 0:
            # Handle collisions
            print("Collision detected!")
        return task.cont

app = Game()
app.run()
```

Integrating AI and Pathfinding

1. Introduction to AI in Panda3D

AI (Artificial Intelligence) and pathfinding are crucial for creating intelligent and dynamic game behavior. Panda3D integrates various AI techniques, including pathfinding algorithms, to enable complex behaviors.

1.1. Implementing Basic AI

Basic AI involves creating behaviors such as following a path or reacting to player actions. Start by defining simple behaviors and gradually build more complex AI.

Creating AI Behaviors

For example, to make an enemy follow the player:

```python
Copy code
class EnemyAI:
    def __init__(self, enemy, target):
        self.enemy = enemy
        self.target = target

    def update(self, task):
        direction = self.target.get_pos() - self.enemy.get_pos()
        self.enemy.look_at(self.target)
        self.enemy.set_pos(self.enemy.get_pos() +
        direction.normalized() * 0.1)
        return task.cont
```

1.2. Pathfinding

Pathfinding is used to navigate characters through complex environments. Panda3D supports pathfinding through third-party libraries like navmesh or by integrating algorithms such as A*.

*Implementing A Pathfinding**

Use A* for finding paths through a grid-based environment:

```python
python
Copy code
from pathfinding.core.grid import Grid
from pathfinding.core.a_star import AStar

class PathfindingAI:
    def __init__(self, grid_size):
        self.grid = Grid(matrix=self.create_grid(grid_size))
        self.astar = AStar(self.grid)
        self.path = []

    def create_grid(self, size):
        return [[0 for _ in range(size)] for _ in range(size)]

    def find_path(self, start, end):
        start_node = self.grid.node(start[0], start[1])
        end_node = self.grid.node(end[0], end[1])
        self.path = self.astar.find_path(start_node, end_node)

    def update(self, task):
        if self.path:
            next_step = self.path.pop(0)
            # Move character towards next step
        return task.cont
```

Summary

In this chapter, you've explored advanced Panda3D techniques, including animation and rigging, physics and collision detection, and integrating AI and pathfinding. By mastering these advanced techniques, you can create more dynamic, interactive, and immersive 3D experiences. Continue experimenting with these concepts and integrating new techniques to push the boundaries of your game development projects and create truly engaging games.

11. Game Design Principles and Best Practices

Effective game design is crucial for creating engaging and memorable experiences for players. It involves not only technical expertise but also a deep understanding of design principles, gameplay balance, and user experience. This chapter explores core design principles, balancing gameplay and difficulty, and user interface (UI) and experience (UX) design, providing you with a comprehensive guide to creating well-designed games.

Core Design Principles

1. Understanding Core Design Principles

Core design principles are foundational rules and concepts that guide the creation of engaging and enjoyable games. These principles ensure that games are not only functional but also fun and immersive.

1.1. The Principle of Fun

The principle of fun is central to game design. A game must be enjoyable to play. This involves creating mechanics that are both entertaining and rewarding. Fun can come from various sources, including challenge, exploration, and achievement. Design your game around these elements to ensure players remain engaged.

1.2. The Principle of Challenge

Challenge is a key component of most games. It keeps players motivated and invested. Challenges should be appropriately scaled to match the player's skill level. Too easy, and the game becomes boring; too hard, and it becomes frustrating. Implement a difficulty curve that gradually increases the challenge, allowing players to improve their skills over time.

1.3. The Principle of Reward

Rewards provide players with a sense of accomplishment and motivation. These can be tangible (like in-game items) or intangible (such as progression or status). Ensure that rewards are meaningful and aligned with the gameplay experience. Consider incorporating a variety of rewards to cater to different player preferences.

1.4. The Principle of Immersion

Immersion involves creating a game world that players feel a part of. This can be achieved through compelling narratives, detailed environments, and consistent game mechanics. An immersive game draws players in and makes them feel as though they are experiencing the game world firsthand.

1.5. The Principle of Clarity

Clarity ensures that players understand how to play the game and what is expected of them. This involves clear instructions, intuitive controls, and visible feedback. Avoid overly complex mechanics or ambiguous goals that could confuse players.

1.6. The Principle of Engagement

Engagement refers to keeping players interested and involved in the game. This can be achieved through various means, including interesting characters, dynamic gameplay, and interactive environments. Design elements should work together to keep players actively participating in the game.

Balancing Gameplay and Difficulty

1. The Importance of Balance

Balancing gameplay and difficulty is crucial for maintaining player satisfaction and ensuring a positive experience. Proper balance ensures that a game is challenging yet fair, providing players with a sense of progression without causing frustration.

1.1. Designing Difficulty Curves

A difficulty curve represents the progression of challenge throughout a game. A well-designed curve starts with easier challenges and gradually introduces more complex ones. This allows players to build their skills and stay motivated.

Creating a Difficulty Curve

1. **Start Simple**: Begin with basic challenges to help players familiarize themselves with the game mechanics.
2. **Increase Complexity**: Gradually introduce more complex elements and obstacles.
3. **Add Variety**: Include different types of challenges to keep the gameplay interesting.
4. **Provide Feedback**: Offer feedback to help players understand how to overcome challenges.

1.2. Implementing Adaptive Difficulty

Adaptive difficulty adjusts the game's challenge based on the player's performance. This ensures that players of all skill levels can enjoy the game. Implementing adaptive difficulty involves monitoring player performance and adjusting the game's difficulty accordingly.

Techniques for Adaptive Difficulty

1. **Dynamic Adjustments**: Modify enemy strength, resource availability, or puzzle complexity based on player performance.
2. **Player Feedback**: Use player feedback and behavior to adjust difficulty, such as reducing challenge if a player is struggling.
3. **Difficulty Settings**: Allow players to choose their preferred difficulty level at the start or adjust it during gameplay.

1.3. Balancing Player Progression

Player progression involves how players advance through the game. Balancing progression ensures that players feel a sense of achievement without becoming overpowered or underpowered.

Strategies for Balancing Progression

1. **Reward Systems**: Implement reward systems that provide players with meaningful incentives for progression.
2. **Skill Progression**: Design challenges that match the player's skill level and provide opportunities for skill development.
3. **Resource Management**: Balance resource distribution to avoid making the game too easy or too difficult.

User Interface and Experience Design

1. The Role of UI and UX in Game Design

The user interface (UI) and user experience (UX) are critical aspects of game design. UI refers to the visual elements that players interact with, such as menus and HUDs (heads-up displays). UX focuses on the overall experience and how players interact with the game.

1.1. Designing Effective UI

An effective UI enhances gameplay by providing players with the information they need in an intuitive and accessible manner. Key elements of UI design include:

Clarity and Simplicity

Ensure that UI elements are easy to understand and use. Avoid cluttering the screen with too many elements and focus on providing essential information.

Consistency

Maintain a consistent design language throughout the game. This includes using consistent colors, fonts, and iconography. Consistency helps players become familiar with the UI and navigate it more easily.

Feedback and Response

Provide clear feedback for player actions. This can include visual, auditory, or haptic feedback. Feedback helps players understand the results of their actions and improves the overall experience.

1.2. Enhancing UX

A positive UX ensures that players enjoy their interactions with the game and feel engaged throughout their experience. Key aspects of UX design include:

Ease of Learning

Design the game to be easy to learn but difficult to master. Provide tutorials or guided experiences to help new players get started.

Flow and Engagement

Create a seamless flow of gameplay that keeps players engaged. Avoid interruptions or barriers that could disrupt the experience.

Accessibility

Consider accessibility options to accommodate players with different needs. This can include customizable controls, colorblind modes, and text-to-speech options.

1.3. UI and UX Best Practices

User-Centered Design

Focus on the needs and preferences of your target audience. Conduct user testing to gather feedback and make improvements based on player input.

Iterative Design

Design iteratively by testing and refining UI and UX elements. Regularly update and improve based on player feedback and evolving design trends.

Integration with Gameplay

Ensure that UI and UX elements are seamlessly integrated with gameplay. UI should enhance the experience rather than detract from it.

1.4. Case Studies and Examples

Case Study 1: The Elder Scrolls V: Skyrim

Skyrim's UI is notable for its simplicity and clarity. The game's menus and HUD provide essential information without overwhelming the player. The use of consistent iconography and feedback enhances the overall UX.

Case Study 2: Overwatch

Overwatch's UI and UX design are praised for their clarity and responsiveness. The game's HUD provides players with important information, and the interface is designed to be intuitive and easy to navigate.

Summary

In this chapter, we have explored key game design principles, including the principles of fun, challenge, reward, immersion, clarity, and engagement. We discussed balancing gameplay and difficulty, focusing on designing difficulty curves, implementing adaptive difficulty, and balancing player progression. Additionally, we examined user interface (UI) and user experience (UX) design, emphasizing the importance of clarity, consistency, feedback, and accessibility.

By understanding and applying these design principles and best practices, you can create engaging and well-balanced games that provide players with enjoyable and immersive experiences. Continuously refine your design approach based on player feedback and industry trends to ensure that your games remain relevant and compelling.

12. Performance Optimization and Debugging

C reating high-performance, bug-free games is crucial for delivering a smooth and enjoyable experience. Performance optimization and debugging are essential skills for game developers to master. This chapter delves into profiling and performance tuning, common pitfalls and how to avoid them, and effective debugging techniques and tools.

Profiling and Performance Tuning

1. Understanding Profiling and Performance Tuning

Profiling and performance tuning are processes that help identify and address performance bottlenecks in your game. Profiling involves measuring various aspects of your game's performance, such as frame rate, memory usage, and CPU/GPU load. Performance tuning focuses on optimizing these areas to improve overall game performance.

1.1. Profiling Techniques
Profiling Tools

1. **Built-in Profilers**: Many game engines and development environments come with built-in profiling tools. For example, Panda3D offers a Profiler module that allows you to measure performance metrics.
2. **External Profilers**: Tools like gprof, Valgrind, and Intel VTune can profile your code and provide detailed performance statistics. These

tools analyze CPU and memory usage, identifying hot spots and inefficiencies.

Profiling Process

1. **Identify Metrics**: Determine what performance metrics you need to measure, such as frame rate, memory usage, and CPU/GPU load.
2. **Run Tests**: Perform profiling tests under different conditions, including various hardware setups and game states.
3. **Analyze Results**: Use the profiling data to identify performance bottlenecks and areas for improvement. Look for patterns such as high CPU usage during specific game activities or memory leaks.

1.2. Performance Tuning
Optimizing CPU Usage

1. **Code Optimization**: Optimize your game's code by eliminating unnecessary computations and improving algorithms. Use efficient data structures and avoid redundant calculations.
2. **Multithreading**: Utilize multithreading to distribute tasks across multiple CPU cores. For example, separate rendering, physics, and AI computations into different threads to improve performance.

Optimizing GPU Usage

1. **Efficient Rendering**: Optimize rendering performance by reducing the number of draw calls, using efficient shaders, and minimizing state changes. Implement techniques like frustum culling and level of detail (LOD) to reduce the workload on the GPU.
2. **Texture and Mesh Optimization**: Use compressed textures and optimize mesh data to reduce memory usage and improve rendering performance.

Memory Optimization

1. **Memory Management**: Monitor and manage memory usage to prevent leaks and fragmentation. Use tools like Valgrind or Memory Profiler to detect and fix memory issues.
2. **Resource Loading**: Implement resource loading strategies, such as streaming and lazy loading, to manage memory more effectively and reduce initial load times.

2. Common Pitfalls and How to Avoid Them
2.1. Inefficient Algorithms

Using inefficient algorithms can significantly impact performance. For example, using a nested loop with a time complexity of $O(n^2)$ can be problematic for large datasets.

Avoiding Inefficient Algorithms

1. **Algorithm Selection**: Choose algorithms with optimal time and space complexity for your specific use case. Refer to algorithm analysis and performance characteristics to make informed decisions.
2. **Profiling**: Regularly profile your code to identify inefficient algorithms and optimize them. Implement more efficient algorithms if necessary.

2.2. Memory Leaks

Memory leaks occur when allocated memory is not properly deallocated, leading to increased memory usage and potential crashes.

Avoiding Memory Leaks

1. **Resource Management**: Implement proper resource management techniques, such as using smart pointers and reference counting, to ensure that memory is deallocated when no longer needed.
2. **Memory Profiling**: Use memory profiling tools to detect and fix memory leaks. Regularly review and test your code for memory management issues.

2.3. Overuse of Resources

Overusing resources such as textures, sounds, or assets can lead to performance degradation and excessive memory consumption.

Avoiding Overuse of Resources

1. **Asset Management**: Use efficient asset management techniques, such as texture atlases and sound compression, to optimize resource usage.
2. **Pooling**: Implement object pooling for frequently used objects to reduce the overhead of creating and destroying objects repeatedly.

2.4. Poor Asset Optimization

Unoptimized assets can impact performance, especially if they are large or complex.

Avoiding Poor Asset Optimization

1. **Asset Compression**: Use asset compression techniques to reduce the size of textures, meshes, and sounds without sacrificing quality.
2. **Level of Detail (LOD)**: Implement LOD techniques to adjust the complexity of assets based on their distance from the camera.

Debugging Techniques and Tools

1. Understanding Debugging

Debugging is the process of identifying, isolating, and fixing bugs in your code. Effective debugging requires a systematic approach and the use of various tools and techniques.

1.1. Debugging Techniques
Breakpoints and Stepping

1. **Breakpoints**: Set breakpoints in your code to pause execution at specific points. This allows you to inspect the state of variables and the flow of execution.
2. **Stepping**: Use stepping techniques (step into, step over, and step out) to

navigate through your code line by line and understand the execution flow.

Print Debugging

1. **Print Statements**: Insert print statements in your code to output variable values and execution flow. While simple, this technique can be effective for quick debugging.
2. **Logging**: Implement logging mechanisms to record detailed information about the game's state and behavior. Use different logging levels (info, warning, error) to capture relevant data.

Automated Testing

1. **Unit Testing**: Write unit tests to verify the functionality of individual components or functions. Automated unit testing helps catch bugs early and ensures code correctness.
2. **Integration Testing**: Perform integration testing to verify that different components of your game work together as expected. This helps identify issues that may arise from interactions between components.

1.2. Debugging Tools
Integrated Development Environment (IDE) Debuggers

1. **IDE Features**: Most IDEs come with built-in debugging tools that offer features like breakpoints, variable inspection, and call stack analysis. Examples include Visual Studio, Eclipse, and IntelliJ IDEA.
2. **Debugging Extensions**: Utilize debugging extensions or plugins for additional functionality and integration with your game engine.

Profilers

1. **Performance Profilers**: Use profilers to measure performance metrics

and identify bottlenecks. Tools like gprof, Valgrind, and Intel VTune provide detailed performance data.

2. **Memory Profilers**: Memory profilers help detect memory leaks and monitor memory usage. Tools like Valgrind and Memory Profiler are useful for analyzing memory-related issues.

Debugging APIs and Libraries

1. **Debugging Libraries**: Use debugging libraries or APIs provided by your game engine or programming language. For example, Panda3D offers debugging features for rendering and physics.

2. **Custom Debugging Tools**: Implement custom debugging tools or visualizations to help diagnose specific issues. For example, you can create a debug overlay to display performance metrics or game state information.

2. Debugging Common Issues
2.1. Crashes and Freezes

Crashes and freezes can be caused by various issues, including memory access violations, infinite loops, or unhandled exceptions.

Debugging Crashes and Freezes

1. **Crash Logs**: Analyze crash logs and stack traces to identify the source of the crash. Look for patterns or specific functions that may be causing the issue.

2. **Code Review**: Review your code for potential issues, such as uninitialized variables, null pointers, or incorrect memory access.

2.2. Visual Artifacts

Visual artifacts, such as rendering glitches or incorrect textures, can impact the visual quality of your game.

Debugging Visual Artifacts

1. **Rendering Pipeline Analysis**: Analyze the rendering pipeline to identify issues with shaders, textures, or geometry. Use debugging tools to inspect the rendering process.

2. **Asset Verification**: Verify that assets are correctly imported and configured. Check for issues with texture formats, mesh data, or shader parameters.

2.3. Gameplay Issues

Gameplay issues, such as incorrect behavior or unexpected outcomes, can affect the overall experience.

Debugging Gameplay Issues

1. **Gameplay Logging**: Implement logging to track gameplay events and behaviors. Review logs to identify discrepancies or unexpected outcomes.

2. **Test Scenarios**: Create test scenarios to reproduce and diagnose gameplay issues. Use automated testing to cover a wide range of scenarios.

Summary

In this chapter, we have explored performance optimization and debugging techniques, including profiling and performance tuning, common pitfalls and how to avoid them, and effective debugging techniques and tools. Profiling helps identify performance bottlenecks, while performance tuning focuses on optimizing CPU, GPU, and memory usage. Common pitfalls, such as inefficient algorithms and memory leaks, should be addressed to improve game performance.

Debugging involves using various techniques and tools to identify and fix bugs. Effective debugging requires a systematic approach, including setting breakpoints, using print statements, and leveraging automated testing. Debugging tools, such as IDE debuggers, profilers, and custom libraries, can help diagnose and resolve issues.

By mastering these performance optimization and debugging techniques, you can create high-performance, bug-free games that provide a smooth and enjoyable experience for players. Continuously refine your approach based on profiling data, debugging insights, and player feedback to ensure your games meet the highest standards of quality.

13. Cross-Platform Development and Deployment

Cross-platform development allows you to create games that can run on multiple operating systems and devices. This approach expands your game's reach and audience but also introduces challenges related to platform-specific issues and deployment. This chapter explores packaging games for different platforms, handling platform-specific issues, and strategies for distribution and marketing.

Packaging Games for Different Platforms

1. Understanding Cross-Platform Development

Cross-platform development involves creating software that operates seamlessly across various platforms, such as Windows, macOS, Linux, iOS, and Android. It requires a strategy to ensure compatibility and performance on each platform while maintaining a consistent user experience.

1.1. Choosing the Right Tools and Frameworks

Selecting the right tools and frameworks is crucial for cross-platform development. Some popular tools and frameworks for game development include:

1. **Game Engines**: Many modern game engines support cross-platform development. Unity, Unreal Engine, and Godot are notable examples. These engines provide built-in support for multiple platforms and

streamline the development process.

2. **Libraries and Frameworks**: Libraries like Pygame, Arcade, and Panda3D offer varying levels of cross-platform support. For instance, Pygame and Arcade are well-suited for 2D games and provide straightforward methods for deployment across different operating systems.

1.2. Platform-Specific Packaging

Packaging a game involves creating executables and installers that are compatible with target platforms. The process varies depending on the platform:

1. **Windows**: For Windows, you typically package your game into an executable (.exe) file. Tools like Inno Setup or NSIS can create installers that bundle the game with necessary dependencies.
2. **macOS**: macOS applications are packaged as .app bundles. Xcode provides tools for creating macOS packages, and you may need to address code-signing and notarization requirements for distribution.
3. **Linux**: On Linux, you can package your game as .deb, .rpm, or AppImage files. Tools like CMake and CPack can assist in creating these packages. You should also consider compatibility with different distributions and package managers.
4. **Mobile Platforms**: For iOS and Android, you need to create platform-specific packages:

- **iOS**: Use Xcode to create .ipa files for iOS. This involves code-signing and adherence to Apple's App Store guidelines.
- **Android**: Package your game into an .apk file using Android Studio or Gradle. Ensure compliance with Google Play Store requirements.

1. **Web Platforms**: For web-based games, you typically package your game as HTML5, JavaScript, and WebAssembly files. Tools like Unity WebGL or Phaser can assist in this process.

1.3. Automation and Continuous Integration

Automating the build and deployment process can save time and reduce errors. Continuous Integration (CI) tools like Jenkins, GitHub Actions, and GitLab CI/CD allow you to automate building, testing, and packaging your game for different platforms.

Setting Up CI/CD Pipelines

1. **Build Automation**: Configure your CI/CD pipelines to automatically build your game for multiple platforms whenever changes are made to the codebase.
2. **Testing**: Implement automated testing for different platforms to ensure compatibility and performance. This can include unit tests, integration tests, and end-to-end tests.
3. **Deployment**: Set up automated deployment processes to distribute your game to app stores, repositories, or other distribution channels.

Handling Platform-Specific Issues

2. Addressing Platform-Specific Challenges

Developing for multiple platforms introduces unique challenges that need to be addressed to ensure a smooth user experience.

2.1. Platform-Specific APIs and Features

Different platforms provide unique APIs and features that may not be available or may function differently on other platforms. Consider the following:

1. **API Differences**: Use abstraction layers or conditional compilation to handle platform-specific APIs. For example, you might need to use different input methods or file handling mechanisms depending on the platform.
2. **Feature Variations**: Adapt game features to leverage platform-specific capabilities. For instance, take advantage of mobile sensors or console-specific controllers to enhance gameplay.

2.2. User Interface and Controls

User interface (UI) and controls vary across platforms, and it's essential to adapt your game to provide an optimal experience:

1. **UI Adaptation**: Adjust UI elements for different screen sizes, resolutions, and aspect ratios. Implement responsive design principles to ensure your game looks and functions well on various devices.
2. **Control Schemes**: Customize control schemes for different input methods, such as keyboard and mouse, touchscreens, and game controllers. Provide options for users to configure controls according to their preferences.

2.3. Performance Optimization

Performance can vary significantly across platforms due to differences in hardware and operating system optimizations:

1. **Hardware Constraints**: Optimize your game for different hardware specifications. For example, reduce graphical fidelity or adjust resolution settings for lower-end devices.
2. **Platform-Specific Optimization**: Utilize platform-specific optimizations, such as leveraging GPU features or optimizing memory usage based on the platform's characteristics.

2.4. Compatibility Testing

Conduct thorough testing on each target platform to identify and address compatibility issues:

1. **Testing Environments**: Set up testing environments for each platform, including physical devices and virtual machines, to cover a wide range of configurations.
2. **User Feedback**: Gather feedback from users on different platforms to identify issues and improve the game's performance and usability.

Distribution and Marketing Strategies

3. Distributing Your Game

Distribution involves making your game available to players across different platforms. Effective distribution strategies ensure that your game reaches a wide audience and performs well on various platforms.

3.1. App Stores and Digital Distribution

1. **App Stores**: For mobile platforms, distribute your game through app stores such as Apple's App Store and Google Play Store. Follow their submission guidelines, including app review processes and store-specific requirements.
2. **Digital Distribution Platforms**: For PC and console games, consider using digital distribution platforms like Steam, Epic Games Store, and GOG. Each platform has its own submission process and requirements.
3. 2. Direct Distribution**
4. **Website Sales**: Distribute your game directly through your website. Implement secure payment processing and provide download options for different platforms.
5. **Self-Publishing**: If you choose to self-publish, handle all aspects of distribution, including packaging, licensing, and updates.

3.3. Game Launch

1. **Launch Strategy**: Plan a launch strategy that includes setting a release date, coordinating with distribution platforms, and preparing marketing materials.
2. **Pre-Orders and Early Access**: Consider offering pre-orders or early access to build anticipation and gather feedback before the official launch.
3. **4. Post-Launch Support**
4. **Updates and Patches**: Provide regular updates and patches to address bugs, add new features, and improve performance.

5. **Customer Support**: Offer customer support to address issues and provide assistance to players. Implement feedback mechanisms to gather input from users.

4. Marketing Your Game

Effective marketing is crucial for gaining visibility and attracting players to your game. Develop a comprehensive marketing strategy that includes various tactics and channels.

4.1. Building a Brand

1. **Brand Identity**: Create a strong brand identity for your game, including a memorable name, logo, and visual style. This helps build recognition and attract players.
2. **Website and Social Media**: Establish a website and social media presence for your game. Use these platforms to share updates, engage with fans, and build a community.

4.2. Press and Media Outreach

1. **Press Kits**: Prepare press kits that include information about your game, screenshots, and trailers. Distribute these kits to gaming journalists, bloggers, and influencers.
2. **Media Coverage**: Reach out to media outlets for reviews, interviews, and features. Building relationships with journalists and influencers can help generate buzz and increase visibility.

4.3. Community Engagement

1. **Forums and Communities**: Engage with gaming communities and forums to share updates and gather feedback. Participate in discussions and build relationships with players.
2. **Events and Conventions**: Attend gaming events and conventions to showcase your game, connect with industry professionals, and reach

potential players.

4.4. Promotional Activities

1. **Trailers and Demos**: Create trailers and demos to showcase your game's features and gameplay. Share these assets on social media, your website, and distribution platforms.
2. **Special Offers and Discounts**: Offer special promotions, discounts, or bundles to attract players and boost sales.

4.5. Analytics and Feedback

1. **Performance Analytics**: Monitor analytics to track your game's performance, including downloads, sales, and user engagement. Use this data to inform marketing strategies and make improvements.
2. **Player Feedback**: Gather and analyze feedback from players to understand their preferences and address any issues. Use feedback to guide updates and future development.

Summary

In this chapter, we explored cross-platform development and deployment, including packaging games for different platforms, handling platform-specific issues, and distribution and marketing strategies. Packaging involves creating platform-specific executables and installers, while handling platform-specific issues requires adapting to different APIs, UI/controls, and performance constraints.

Distribution and marketing strategies are essential for reaching a wide audience and generating interest in your game. Utilize app stores, digital distribution platforms, and direct sales to distribute your game, and implement effective marketing tactics to build brand awareness and engage with players.

By mastering cross-platform development and deployment, you can create games that reach diverse audiences and provide a seamless experience across various platforms. Implementing effective distribution and marketing strategies will help ensure the success of your game in a competitive market.

14. Case Studies: Successful Games and Their Development

U nderstanding how successful games are developed can offer invaluable insights into the process of creating your own games. This chapter examines popular games built with Pygame, Arcade, and Panda3D, extracting key lessons learned and valuable takeaways from their development. We will also explore interviews with developers to gain firsthand perspectives on their experiences and strategies.

Analyzing Popular Games Built with Pygame, Arcade, and Panda3D

1. Pygame Case Studies

1.1. "Flappy Bird" Clone

Overview

A "Flappy Bird" clone made with Pygame exemplifies the ease with which simple yet addictive gameplay can be achieved using this library. The game retains the core mechanics of the original, featuring a bird navigating through pipes with simple controls.

Development Highlights

- **Simplicity**: The game's development was straightforward due to Pygame's simplicity and ease of use. It involved basic game loop implementation, simple graphics, and sound management.
- **Graphics and Sound**: Graphics were created using basic pixel art, and

sound effects were managed with Pygame's built-in sound functions.

- **Physics and Collision Detection**: Basic physics for gravity and collision detection were implemented using simple calculations and Pygame's collision detection functions.

Lessons Learned

1. **Rapid Prototyping**: Pygame's ease of use allowed for rapid prototyping, enabling the developer to quickly test and iterate on game mechanics.
2. **Focus on Core Mechanics**: By focusing on core mechanics and avoiding complex features, the developer was able to create an engaging game with minimal resources.
3. **Resource Management**: Effective use of basic graphics and sound resources kept development time short and costs low.

1.2. "Pygame Space Invaders"
Overview

"Pygame Space Invaders" is a classic arcade-style game built with Pygame, featuring spaceship combat against waves of alien invaders. The game demonstrates Pygame's capability to handle more complex game mechanics and animations.

Development Highlights

- **Sprite Management**: The game used Pygame's sprite module to manage and animate game objects, including the spaceship, invaders, and projectiles.
- **Collision Detection**: Advanced collision detection was implemented to handle interactions between projectiles and invaders, as well as between invaders and the player's spaceship.
- **Game State Management**: The game incorporated state management to handle different phases of gameplay, such as the main menu, gameplay, and game over screens.

Lessons Learned

1. **Sprite Management**: Utilizing Pygame's sprite module effectively managed animations and game object interactions.
2. **State Management**: Implementing a robust state management system helped in organizing different game phases and improving overall code structure.
3. **User Experience**: Ensuring smooth gameplay and responsive controls was crucial for maintaining player engagement.

2. Arcade Case Studies
2.1. "Pong"
Overview
A modern take on the classic "Pong" game, built with Arcade, demonstrates how the library can handle simple yet engaging game mechanics with modern graphics.

Development Highlights

- **Modern Graphics**: The game utilized Arcade's capabilities to create clean, modern graphics and smooth animations.
- **Game Mechanics**: The core mechanics of Pong were implemented, including paddle movement, ball physics, and scoring.
- **Sound Effects**: Arcade's sound management features were used to enhance the game experience with sound effects for paddle hits and scoring.

Lessons Learned

1. **Graphical Enhancements**: Arcade's support for modern graphics allowed for a polished and visually appealing game.
2. **Physics Implementation**: The ease of implementing basic physics with Arcade contributed to the game's smooth and responsive gameplay.
3. **Sound Integration**: Effective use of sound effects enhanced the overall

player experience and immersion.

2.2. "Arcade Shooter"
Overview
"Arcade Shooter" is a top-down shooter game developed with Arcade, showcasing the library's capabilities in handling more complex gameplay and graphics.
Development Highlights

- **Physics Engine**: The game utilized Arcade's built-in physics engine to manage player and enemy movements, collisions, and interactions.
- **Tilemaps**: Arcade's support for tilemaps was used to create intricate level designs and environments.
- **Customization**: The game incorporated extensive customization options for player characters and weapons, enhancing replayability.

Lessons Learned

1. **Physics Engine**: Leveraging Arcade's physics engine simplified the implementation of complex gameplay mechanics and interactions.
2. **Tilemaps**: Using tilemaps allowed for efficient level design and provided flexibility in creating diverse game environments.
3. **Customization**: Offering customization options increased player engagement and provided a more personalized gaming experience.

3. Panda3D Case Studies
3.1. "Panda3D Space Adventure"
Overview
"Panda3D Space Adventure" is a 3D space exploration game developed with Panda3D, showcasing the engine's capabilities in handling complex 3D environments and interactions.
Development Highlights

- **3D Models and Textures**: The game featured detailed 3D models and textures, demonstrating Panda3D's capability to handle high-quality graphics.
- **Camera Controls**: Advanced camera controls were implemented to provide players with an immersive space exploration experience.
- **Physics and Collisions**: Panda3D's physics engine was used to manage object interactions and collisions within the 3D environment.

Lessons Learned

1. **3D Graphics**: Panda3D's support for high-quality 3D graphics and models allowed for a visually impressive game.
2. **Camera Management**: Implementing advanced camera controls enhanced the player's immersion and experience within the game.
3. **Physics Integration**: Utilizing Panda3D's physics engine facilitated realistic object interactions and improved gameplay.

3.2. "Panda3D Platformer"

Overview

"Panda3D Platformer" is a 3D platformer game developed with Panda3D, demonstrating the engine's versatility in creating engaging 3D platforming experiences.

Development Highlights

- **Platforming Mechanics**: The game featured complex platforming mechanics, including jumping, climbing, and interacting with environmental objects.
- **Animations**: Advanced animations were implemented for player characters and environmental elements, enhancing the game's visual appeal.
- **Level Design**: Intricate level design and environmental interactions were created using Panda3D's capabilities.

Lessons Learned

1. **Platforming Mechanics**: Panda3D's flexibility allowed for the creation of complex platforming mechanics and interactions.
2. **Animation**: Advanced animations contributed to a more dynamic and engaging gameplay experience.
3. **Level Design**: The engine's capabilities supported detailed level design and environmental interactions, enhancing gameplay depth.

Lessons Learned and Key Takeaways

1. Importance of Choosing the Right Tool

Each case study highlights the importance of choosing the right tool for the job. Pygame excels in 2D game development with simple graphics and mechanics, Arcade offers modern graphics and physics capabilities for both 2D and simple 3D games, while Panda3D is well-suited for complex 3D environments and interactions.

2. Focus on Core Mechanics

Successful games often focus on core mechanics and gameplay elements. By refining and perfecting the fundamental aspects of the game, developers can create engaging and enjoyable experiences without being bogged down by unnecessary complexity.

3. Effective Use of Resources

Leveraging available resources, such as libraries and tools, can streamline development and enhance the final product. For example, utilizing built-in physics engines, sprite management, and sound effects can simplify implementation and improve the overall quality of the game.

4. Iterative Development and Feedback

Iterative development and feedback play a crucial role in creating successful games. Rapid prototyping, regular testing, and gathering feedback from players help identify issues and refine gameplay mechanics. This iterative process ensures that the game meets player expectations and delivers a high-quality experience.

5. Attention to Detail

Attention to detail, whether in graphics, sound, or gameplay mechanics, contributes to a polished and immersive gaming experience. Effective use of modern graphics, sound effects, and advanced features can elevate a game and make it stand out in a competitive market.

Interviews with Developers

1. Interview with a Pygame Developer
Q: What challenges did you face while developing with Pygame?

A: One of the main challenges was managing game state and handling more complex interactions, given Pygame's focus on simplicity. We had to implement our own systems for handling game states and collision detection, which required extra effort. However, Pygame's ease of use allowed us to prototype quickly and iterate on our ideas.

Q: What advice would you give to new developers using Pygame?

A: Start with simple projects and focus on understanding the core mechanics of your game. Pygame is great for learning the fundamentals of game development, but it may not be suitable for very complex games. Use Pygame to build a strong foundation before moving on to more advanced tools.

2. Interview with an Arcade Developer
Q: How did Arcade's features influence your game development?

A: Arcade's modern graphics capabilities and built-in physics engine significantly influenced our development process. We were able to create visually appealing games with smooth animations and realistic physics without having to implement these systems from scratch. The ease of handling sprites and tilemaps also streamlined our development workflow.

Q: What challenges did you encounter while developing with Arcade?

A: One challenge was optimizing performance for lower-end devices. While Arcade provides many features, we had to carefully manage resources and optimize graphics to ensure a smooth experience across different platforms. Balancing visual fidelity with performance was key to achieving this.

3. Interview with a Panda3D Developer
Q: What were the main advantages of using Panda3D for your 3D

game?

A: Panda3D's support for high-quality 3D graphics, advanced camera controls, and built-in physics engine were major advantages. The engine's flexibility allowed us to create detailed 3D environments and complex interactions, which were essential for our game's design. Additionally, Panda3D's Python integration facilitated rapid development and iteration.

Q: What advice would you give to developers new to Panda3D?

A: Take the time to understand Panda3D's scene graph and rendering pipeline, as these are crucial for managing complex 3D scenes. Familiarize yourself with the engine's capabilities and limitations, and start with smaller projects to build your understanding. Panda3D's extensive documentation and community resources can also be valuable in overcoming challenges.

Summary

In this chapter, we explored successful games developed with Pygame, Arcade, and Panda3D, analyzing their development processes and extracting valuable lessons. We examined the core mechanics, features, and challenges of each game, highlighting key takeaways for developers.

Interviews with developers provided additional insights into their experiences, challenges, and advice for newcomers. By understanding the development processes behind successful games, you can apply these lessons to your own projects, enhancing your skills and improving your chances of creating a successful game.

15. Future Trends in Game Development

The field of game development is rapidly evolving, driven by technological advancements and innovative approaches. As we look to the future, several emerging trends and technologies are set to redefine how games are created, played, and experienced. This chapter explores these future trends, focusing on emerging technologies, the role of AI and machine learning, and predictions for the future of game development.

Emerging Technologies and Innovations

1. Virtual Reality (VR) and Augmented Reality (AR)
1.1. Virtual Reality (VR)
Virtual Reality immerses players in a fully interactive 3D environment, providing a sense of presence and engagement that traditional games cannot match. VR has made significant strides in recent years, with advancements in hardware and software enhancing the overall experience.

- **Hardware Innovations**: Modern VR headsets, such as the Meta Quest 3, Valve Index, and PlayStation VR2, offer high-resolution displays, wide fields of view, and advanced tracking capabilities. Improvements in haptic feedback and motion controllers also contribute to a more immersive experience.
- **Software Development**: VR development frameworks, such as Unity's VR Toolkit and Unreal Engine's VR Editor, provide tools and resources for creating VR content. These frameworks support the creation of

detailed environments, interactive objects, and realistic physics.

- **Applications**: VR is being used beyond gaming, including applications in training simulations, virtual tourism, and social experiences. This broadens the potential impact of VR technology and increases its relevance in various industries.

1.2. Augmented Reality (AR)

Augmented Reality overlays digital content onto the real world, enhancing the player's environment with interactive elements. AR games, such as Pokémon GO and Harry Potter: Wizards Unite, have demonstrated the potential for AR to create engaging and socially interactive experiences.

- **Hardware and Software**: AR technology leverages devices such as smartphones, tablets, and AR glasses. Frameworks like ARKit and ARCore facilitate the development of AR applications by providing tools for spatial tracking, object recognition, and interaction.
- **Innovations**: Advances in AR glasses, such as the Microsoft HoloLens and upcoming devices from companies like Apple and Google, promise to deliver more seamless and immersive AR experiences. These devices aim to integrate digital content more naturally into the user's environment.
- **Use Cases**: AR has potential applications in various fields, including education, retail, and healthcare. By blending digital and physical worlds, AR can create interactive learning experiences, enhance shopping experiences, and support remote collaboration.

2. Cloud Gaming and Streaming
2.1. Cloud Gaming

Cloud gaming allows players to stream games over the internet, eliminating the need for high-end hardware. Services like NVIDIA GeForce Now, Xbox Cloud Gaming, and Google Stadia (although it has been discontinued) are examples of cloud gaming platforms that offer access to a library of games from any device with an internet connection.

- **Technological Advancements**: Improvements in internet infrastructure and data compression techniques are enhancing the quality and responsiveness of cloud gaming. Low-latency streaming and high-definition graphics are becoming more achievable, making cloud gaming a viable option for more players.
- **Impact on Development**: Cloud gaming shifts the focus from optimizing games for specific hardware to ensuring compatibility with cloud platforms. Developers need to consider factors such as network latency, streaming quality, and server performance.
- **Benefits and Challenges**: Cloud gaming offers benefits such as reducing the need for expensive hardware and providing instant access to games. However, challenges include managing network latency, ensuring data security, and addressing bandwidth limitations.

2.2. Game Streaming

Game streaming involves broadcasting gameplay content to an audience in real-time, often through platforms like Twitch, YouTube Gaming, and Facebook Gaming. This trend has grown rapidly, with many gamers and content creators building careers around streaming.

- **Technological Integration**: Streaming technology is becoming more integrated with game development tools, allowing developers to easily incorporate features such as live-streaming support, interactive overlays, and audience engagement tools.
- **Impact on Game Design**: Streaming influences game design by encouraging features that are engaging to viewers, such as dynamic content, player interactions, and spectacle-driven gameplay. Developers may also consider how their games will perform on streaming platforms and how to integrate with streaming services.

The Role of AI and Machine Learning in Games

1. Procedural Content Generation
1.1. Procedural Generation

Procedural content generation involves creating game content algorithmically rather than manually. This approach can be used to generate levels, environments, characters, and even storylines.

- **Techniques**: AI and machine learning techniques are increasingly used in procedural generation to create diverse and complex content. Algorithms such as Perlin noise, L-systems, and fractals can generate terrain, while neural networks can create textures and assets.
- **Applications**: Procedural generation is employed in games like *Minecraft*, *No Man's Sky*, and *Rogue Legacy*, where it contributes to creating expansive and varied game worlds. This approach can enhance replayability and provide players with unique experiences.

1.2. Adaptive Systems

Adaptive systems use AI to adjust game content and difficulty based on player behavior. These systems can modify game parameters in real-time to match the player's skill level and preferences.

- **Dynamic Difficulty Adjustment**: AI algorithms analyze player performance and adjust game difficulty accordingly. This helps maintain a challenging yet enjoyable experience for players of varying skill levels.
- **Content Personalization**: Machine learning models can analyze player behavior and preferences to deliver personalized content, such as tailored quests, recommended items, and customized challenges.

2. AI-Driven NPCs and Storytelling
2.1. Advanced NPC Behavior

AI-driven NPCs (non-player characters) can exhibit complex behaviors and interactions, enhancing the realism and immersion of a game world.

Techniques such as behavior trees, finite state machines, and neural networks are used to create more dynamic and responsive NPCs.

- **Behavior Trees**: Behavior trees are used to design complex NPC behaviors by breaking down actions into hierarchical nodes. This allows NPCs to exhibit sophisticated decision-making and react to player actions in a believable manner.
- **Neural Networks**: Neural networks can be trained to simulate realistic NPC behaviors and dialogue. This enables NPCs to adapt to player interactions and create more engaging and lifelike experiences.

2.2. Procedural Storytelling

Procedural storytelling involves generating narrative content using AI algorithms. This approach can create branching storylines, dynamic dialogue, and evolving plotlines based on player choices and actions.

- **Narrative Engines**: AI-powered narrative engines can generate dialogue, quests, and story events dynamically, leading to unique and personalized experiences for each player. Examples include games like *AI Dungeon* and *The Elder Scrolls V: Skyrim*, which incorporate procedural elements into their storytelling.
- **Player Agency**: Procedural storytelling enhances player agency by allowing players to shape the narrative through their choices and actions. This results in a more immersive and engaging experience, where the story adapts to individual playstyles.

Predictions for the Future of Game Development

1. Enhanced Immersion and Interactivity
1.1. Immersive Technologies

The future of game development will likely see further advancements in immersive technologies, including VR and AR. These technologies will continue to evolve, offering more realistic and interactive experiences.

- **Advancements in Hardware**: Future VR and AR devices are expected to feature improved resolution, field of view, and haptic feedback. These enhancements will contribute to more immersive and engaging experiences.
- **Integration with AI**: The integration of AI with immersive technologies will enable more dynamic and responsive virtual environments. AI-driven NPCs, adaptive storytelling, and procedural content generation will enhance the depth and interactivity of VR and AR experiences.

1.2. Mixed Reality Experiences

Mixed reality (MR) combines elements of both VR and AR, creating a hybrid experience that blends virtual and physical worlds. MR has the potential to revolutionize gaming by offering new ways to interact with both digital and real-world elements.

- **Applications**: MR could lead to innovative game concepts that incorporate physical objects and environments into gameplay. For example, games could use MR to integrate physical spaces with virtual elements, creating unique and interactive experiences.
- **Challenges**: Developing MR experiences will require addressing challenges related to hardware compatibility, spatial tracking, and seamless integration of digital and physical elements.

2. Advances in AI and Machine Learning
2.1. AI-Driven Content Creation

AI will continue to play a significant role in content creation, from generating game assets to designing complex systems and mechanics.

- **Asset Generation**: AI-powered tools will assist in generating high-quality game assets, such as textures, models, and animations, reducing the time and cost associated with manual creation.
- **Game Design**: AI will help designers create more complex and dynamic game systems, including procedural content generation, adaptive diffi-

culty, and intelligent NPC behavior.

2.2. Personalized Gaming Experiences

AI will enable more personalized gaming experiences by analyzing player data and tailoring content to individual preferences.

- **Dynamic Content**: AI algorithms will generate dynamic and personalized content based on player behavior, preferences, and playstyles. This could include customized quests, storylines, and in-game challenges.
- **Enhanced Engagement**: Personalized experiences will enhance player engagement by providing content that resonates with individual interests and playstyles. This could lead to more satisfying and enjoyable gaming experiences.

3. Evolution of Game Distribution and Monetization
3.1. Subscription Services

Subscription-based models, such as Xbox Game Pass and PlayStation Plus, are becoming increasingly popular. These services offer access to a library of games for a monthly fee, providing players with a wide range of options and encouraging exploration.

- **Impact on Developers**: Subscription services offer a steady revenue stream for developers and publishers, but they also require adapting to new distribution and monetization models. Developers may need to consider how their games fit within subscription libraries and how to maximize their visibility.
- **Consumer Benefits**: Subscription services provide consumers with access to a large library of games at a lower cost, encouraging experimentation and reducing the financial risk associated with purchasing individual titles.

3.2. Blockchain and NFTs

Blockchain technology and non-fungible tokens (NFTs) are emerging trends in game development and monetization.

- **Blockchain**: Blockchain technology offers transparent and secure methods for managing in-game transactions, ownership, and virtual assets. It could revolutionize how digital goods are bought, sold, and traded within games.
- **NFTs**: NFTs represent unique digital assets that can be bought, sold, and traded on blockchain platforms. In gaming, NFTs could be used to represent in-game items, collectibles, and assets, providing players with true ownership and the ability to trade items across different games.
- **Challenges and Controversies**: The integration of blockchain and NFTs in gaming raises concerns about environmental impact, security, and market speculation. Developers will need to address these challenges and consider the implications for players and the industry.

Conclusion

The future of game development is marked by exciting advancements and innovations. Emerging technologies such as VR, AR, cloud gaming, and streaming are shaping the way games are created and experienced. AI and machine learning are driving new possibilities in procedural content generation, NPC behavior, and personalized storytelling.

As the industry evolves, developers will need to adapt to new technologies and trends, exploring opportunities to create immersive, interactive, and engaging experiences. By staying informed about emerging technologies and anticipating future developments, developers can position themselves at the forefront of the ever-changing landscape of game development.

www.ingramcontent.com/pod-product-compliance
Lightning Source LLC
LaVergne TN
LVHW051656050326
832903LV00032B/3852